The Best of Baltimore Beauties

95 Patterns for Album Blocks and Borders

ELLY SIENKIEWICZ

C&T PUBLISHING

Developmental Editor: Cyndy Lyle Rymer
Technical Editors: Barbara Konzak Kuhn and Diane Pedersen
Copy Editor: Steven Cook
Book Design: Rose Sheifer
Cover: Aliza Kahn
Production Assistant: Kirstie L. McCormick
Graphic Illustrations for new patterns and icons: Amante Quias,
   Rose Sheifer and Claudia Boehm
Cover Images: Photos by Sharon Riesdorph
Front Cover: "Basket of Flowers" by Elly Sienkiewicz

Black and white photographs from *Baltimore Album Quilts* and *Baltimore
Beauties and Beyond, Vol. II* are reprinted courtesy of: Sotheby's Photography
Studio, New York (pages 17, 18, 25, 59, 64, 69, 81, 85, 89, 97); Sharon Risedorph
(pages 12, 15, 16, 27, 29, 33, 51, 55, 93); and G.D. Garrison (page 13, 14, 47).

Attention Teachers:
C&T Publishing, Inc. encourages you to use this book as a text for
teaching. Contact us at 800-284-1114 or www.ctpub.com for more
information about the C&T Teachers Program.

Library of Congress Cataloging-in-Publication Data

Sienkiewicz, Elly.
  The best of Baltimore beauties :95 pattern for album blocks and
borders / Elly Sienkiewicz.
      p. cm.
Includes index.
  ISBN 1-57120-086-X (paper trade)
1. Appliqué—Patterns. 2. Album quilts—Maryland—Baltimore.
3. Patchwork—Patterns. I. Title.
TT779 .S5424 1999
746.46'041—dc21
                        99-050545

Published by C&T Publishing, Inc.
P.O. Box 1456
Lafayette, California 94549

Printed in China
10 9 8 7 6 5 4 3 2

Contents

Lyre   Floral   Fruit   Album   Wreath   Birds   Basket   Border   Heart

Papercut   Vase   Music   Cornucopia   House   Ship   Frame   Tree   Patriotic

Contents (continued)

Contents (continued)

PAPERCUTS AND PLENTY

NEW PATTERNS

This book is dedicated to Eleanor Naomi Sienkiewicz
who was born May 5,1999 to my dearest daughter-in-law
Katja Hock Sienkiewicz and my own first born,
Donald Hamilton Sienkiewicz.

Little Ellie,
Sweet Golden Smile of a Soul,
Beloved,
I thank you for making my childhood dream of
being a grandmother come true. Soon, so soon—when you
learn to walk and talk—we will sit and stitch and tell each other
stories! In the meantime, now and
forever, I whisper in your ear and your
laughter dances in my heart.

ACKNOWLEDGMENTS
Thank you, each one who has made the
Baltimore Beauties series possible.
These books—and they whom these books have brought
into my life—give me joy.

Preface

Beyond Baltimore—Because It Matters

When a modern (you or I) entered the vintage realm of Baltimore's Albums, she crossed ring after ring of quilt genres, each more splendid and interesting than that which she had met before. She was used to greatness of scale, having resonated to patiently pieced Log Cabin quilts, constellations of Lone Stars, the nostalgia of Grandmothers' Flower Gardens, the sheer mass of humble Nine-patches. She had witnessed devout dreams clothed in white-on-white, then quilted, stuffed, and brought to life. She had felt awe at block names witness to panoramic history (Rake, Kansas' Troubles, Delectable Mountains) by which courageous quiltmakers—forgers of our nation—had stitched their soul to hers. And yet, after passing through America's most monumental needle-work, she was impressed above all by appliqué, an art of infinite expanse, the end of which she could not see, no matter in which direction she looked.

For over 150 years the appliqué art embodied in antebellum Album Quilts has floated at the peak of quiltmakers' imaginations. Unlike Baltimore—the city that gave these quilts her name—the who? why? how? of these magical quilts had vanished just beyond memory. But no more. Now those original quilts have been eclipsed by these, our contemporary Albums, made not with overweening ambition, but with the greatest humility, and on a quiet womanly scale, and in caring homes, and as the cradle of simple gifts.

This Baltimore Album Revival was not expected to be what it became. It was expected to be infinite-seeming in artistry recognized, techniques revealed, history shared, women's lives affirmed; not in hundreds of quilts, thousands of blocks, dimensional flowers piling a quarter of a mile high, and thread stitched so doggedly that, did it so aspire, it could wrap our Planet Earth 'round and 'round and 'round again. It was expected to be a revival of unfathomable numbers, but in unfathomable numbers of leaves and stems and bows and berries rather than of masterpiece quilts, boundless squares, Baltimore block-carrying cases, masters' classes, stitching groups, appliqué guilds, burning enthusiasms, and stitchers across the world joined through and through by shared joy and silent understanding.

Nonetheless, this current great inventory of quilts, blocks, books, teachers, class-takers, burgeoning technique, lives recorded, friendships cemented, and quiltmakers bound by community is what we now have. A Revival founded according to a vision of individually created beauty has become a sub-culture. A Revival founded in humble aspirations has become a movement of substantial power.

When the Baltimore Album Revival was 1980s young, our modern stitcher studied the classic quilts, searching out the secrets in their symbols and the clues in their history. Ostensibly she sought to learn the quilts' artistry and technology that she herself might follow their needlework journey. Today we have watched that Album style well. We've seen its techniques so clearly that the best contemporary quilts equal or surpass in greatness each and every one of the classic models that we had aproached in awe. But all that remains uniquely "Baltimore" in those old quilts still matters: We have not forgotten their high qualities of thought, their unerring sense of balance, their warmth of character, their joyous patriotism, their optimism, their steady faithfulness, and their idyllic intent. Though we stitch in a style now "beyond Baltimore" we have accumulated rich stores from the Old Ones' beauty and decency. Our moral thirst, a thirst ever-slaked by the Album's nobility, maintains a Baltimore Album Revival still vital as our old century becomes the new. In this vast Universe that is our home, we hunger to know that who we are and what we do matters. Baltimore's Albums are a wellspring of warmth which reassure us that this is so.

The human lessons taught through Baltimore's vintage Album Quilts are a sacred trust. This trust must keep us humble though our needles now sing with siren-like skill. For in those antique Albums we met people who did without, who toiled and sacrificed, women who kept civility while the Industrial Revolution redefined their lives, women who hugged good-bye to children headed West by rail or east by clippership and steamer, women who lost loved ones to seas braved, to war waged, and to the building of a nation—women like ourselves whose cares were no less than our own. Baltimore's Album ledger records "America's hard-earned accounts—the principles we established, the battles we fought, the morals we upheld for century after century, our very humility before God." Like blood in the sand, this legacy has been squandered today by some in a generation "which imagines history to be but a prelude to its own ambitions."

Yet this betrayal by weak souls will not be the end of things, for, history tells us, Principles are eternal. "They simply wait to be called," writes Mark Halprin in *Imprimus* (4/1998). "They arise as if of their own accord when in the face of danger natural courage comes into play and honor and defiance are born. Things such as courage and honor can be neglected, but they cannot be lost.... [they] rise to the occasion." In the stitching of Albums lies a discipline that pulls you to an immense earth-bound task and keeps you there, makes you diligent, like a farmer whose day holds twelve hours of straight furrows to plow. The magnitude of the effort involved—and the certainty that your quilt will stand as testament long after your own mortality—makes you transcend yourself. The mantle of Legacy Album Quiltmaker carries the weight of history, the accomplishments of your predecessors, and keeps you humble. Coupled with real skill, this sobriety and care allows you to put more into your new quilt, even, than you have received from the old. And so the gift goes on.

Each of our lives hangs in a balance between good and evil, joy and sorrow, sickness and health. We should live, as Winston Churchill wrote, "in a continual stress of soul." We cherish peace, but fear its fragility. We are grateful for days blessed with well-being and happiness, knowing that their counterparts will reappear as surely as dusk follows dawn. We are not innocent. But we can lift our hearts in gratitude for food, friends, family, a roof over our heads, and love of each other and our country. We can choose, as Voltaire suggested we must, to "cultivate our gardens." We can choose to stitch eternal optimism into our quilts. Making an Album Quilt is an act of integrity and courage. It is a providential gift given to us in times of need. You and I aspire to stitch immortal beauty into our lives. You will see that contemporary quiltmakers have done just that. Amazingly! To all you who have finished a Revivalist Baltimore, our souls accept your beauty-gift with greatest pleasure. And we thank you for that good gift, from the bottoms of our hearts!

Editor's Note: This preface is based on the author's Opening Address given at the Awards Ceremony of C&T Publishing's Baltimore Album Legacy Show at Santa Clara, CA, October, 1998. Audience members requested that this address be published. To preface this compendium of patterns from Baltimore Beauties and Beyond seemed the ideal place to do so.

Introduction

It was love at first sight. Viewing antique quilts on exhibition, I, all unexpecting, found soulmates. Those Old Ones (circa 1844-1854) were boldly bright; almost flashy. Beauties they were; fascinating, but not my type. A tear brimmed in my eye. It puzzled me, for I did not know then that they were slipping into my soul. That was 1982 and now, eighteen years later, I still love the antebellum Baltimore quilt style and its "beyond Baltimore" descendants. In 1982, though, practicality ruled my life: I mothered three children and managed two businesses. Bone tired, I struggled to be free of the businesses. Philosophical by nature, I had not asked a profound question for five years—since my youngest had been born. Entrepreneurship and motherhood were in eclipse, I struggled to regain balance—and happiness. Who would have thought Albums would be my way?

Summer, 1982, I drafted Album block patterns for my mail-order quilt supply catalogue and came to know these quilts better. Compelling, those patterns became my first book, *Spoken Without a Word, A Lexicon of Symbols in Baltimore's Album Quilts with 24 Faithfully Reproduced Block Patterns*. Next I sold the mail-order company and took up writing the *Baltimore Beauties,* a Baltimore Album Quilt history and how-to series. Producing those books was a devotion and a joy. A bit to my surprise, they readily found an affirming audience. In the last decades of the twentieth century, appliquéing blocks for Revivalist Baltimores became an international movement; one fueled by devoted teachers and a thriving quilt industry. The Baltimores are for almost everyone. They remain a meadow of flowers to be plucked by those wishing to learn appliqué. As a design and inspiration source they are inexhaustible. Many who have completed Baltimore quilts intend to continue their Album journey happily into the sunset. And I who have stitched dozens of quilts in blocks, find these vintage Albums a fertile field for ever-changing dreams—even as the old century turns to the new.

The Best of Baltimore Beauties has been published to serve the twenty-first century quiltmaker embarked on the Album Quilt journey. It is a compendium of patterns from my *Baltimore Album Quilts, Dimensional Appliqué, Baltimore Beauties and Beyond, Volume II, Papercuts and Plenty, Spoken Without a Word*, and a handful of my previously unpublished patterns. Each pattern is keyed to how-to lessons in *Baltimore Beauties and Beyond, Volume I.* Lesson by lesson, in informative increments, *Volume I* leads from the most basic one-layer appliqué on to appliqué mastery. It demystifies the making of a complex classic quilt style, and *The Best of Baltimore* will serve *Volume I's* readers as an excellent source of further patterns. Other than *Volume I,* the *Beauties* books (listed in About the Author on page 224) are out of print. Should you seek one, the most likely source is the auction site, E-bay, or elsewhere on the internet.

This Book's Format

The Best of Baltimore Beauties' patterns are grouped by the book in which they first appeared. Their numbers and graphic presentation are excerpted from their original books. You'll hear the tone of the pattern notes vary from book to book as I tried, for example, to convey historic background in *Baltimore Album Quilts* and focused on fabric manipulation in *Dimensional Appliqué.* Beyond being keyed to how-to lessons in *Volume I,* each pattern's historical context is set by the following designations:

Beyond Baltimore means beyond mid-nineteenth century Baltimore in time or place. These may be either old blocks in a style associated with Baltimore or contemporary blocks in Baltimore-style. If contemporary, the design is my original or that of a named contributor.

Classic Baltimore means a quilt or block pattern taken from a Baltimore Album Quilt of the mid-nineteenth century. A quilt is an authentic Baltimore Album Quilt if inscribed (or placed by provenance) with the geographic location Baltimore and a date between 1844 and 1856.

Baltimore-Style means a quilt or block pattern that looks as though it might originate in a mid-nineteenth century Baltimore Album Quilt but whose provenance is uncertain. This term is also used for contemporary work recognizably related to the style of old Baltimore.

HOW TO TAKE A PATTERN FROM THIS BOOK

Baltimore Beauties and Beyond, Volume I (1989) originated a pattern transfer system whereby a 12½" pattern square could be presented at a set fraction of the whole pattern per book page. A 12½" (block size) square of freezer paper is folded into quadrants, shiny side inside, and the pattern is traced onto the paper's flat side, unit by unit. This "quadrant" pattern transfer method has now become the norm for quilt magazines and books. Within each book excerpt, the *Best of Baltimore* patterns follow the sequence of patterns presented at one eighth (two per pattern page), up to patterns presented by four quadrants on four pattern pages, last. For complete pattern transfer instruction, see "Pattern Transfer" in *Volume I,* pages 21-25. If you are familiar with that method, the following summary should suffice:

Patterns presented at ⅛ or ¼: Papercut (snowflake) patterns are cut from a 12½" paper square folded into eighths, much as school children scissors-cut

snowflakes. Such patterns can be appliquéd from a single layer of cloth. In this sense they are the simplest of Baltimore's block designs. But because, like snowflakes, the designs can be complex, some of them can also be a challenge to stitch! By separating one element, say the blossoms, from a papercut pattern, it can be appliquéd in two layers.

Hint: After folding the 12½" square of freezer paper into eighths, mark the center (where the folds meet) with a C for center. Mark the point where the hypotenuse meets the raw edges with an E for edge. Mark C and E on the top side of the folded paper. Then turn it over and mark the underside of the paper. When you open the paper, you can trace the pattern fraction onto either of the two wedges marked C/E, knowing that they will be on the outside when you refold and staple the paper prior to cutting its pattern. Use repositionable tape to hold the paper in place (matching Cs and Es) over the book as you trace.

Patterns presented at ½ of the block, by two pattern pages: These patterns are first traced onto a 12½" square of freezer paper folded into quarters and marked C and E as above. The full block diagram shows you which half of the pattern is presented as quadrants #1 and #2. Trace the pattern onto the first folded freezer paper quadrant and then the second. Staple, then cut the pattern out double on-the-fold.

Patterns presented at ¼ of the block, by four pattern pages: These patterns are first traced onto a 12½" square of freezer paper folded into quarters. The full block diagram shows you which quarter to trace from which pattern page and numbers their tracing sequence.

Separate pattern elements: Basket patterns to be traced on the fold, then cut-out double, are stacked several to a page. Because baskets, urns, and vases invite you to customize their contents, these patterns are included for inspiration but without a full block drawing.

SUPPLEMENTARY RESOURCES FOR *THE BEST OF BALTIMORE BEAUTIES*

Baltimore Beauties and Beyond, Volume I remains the essential manual for learning Baltimore Album appliqué. For further details on basic appliqué in general, you'll appreciate *Appliqué 12 Easy Ways!* winner of the Quilt Industry Classics Best Appliqué Book Award. Its sequel, *Fancy Appliqué, 12 Lessons to Enhance Your Skills* does just what its subtitle promises. All three of these technique books are published by C&T Publishing. Always looking for a fresh approach, I've been exploring the Album fancywork and my recent designs are pictured in *The Best of Baltimore's* cover photos. The front cover's Basket of Flowers pattern from *Spoken Without a Word* appears on pages 211–212. Instructions for the cover picture's Ribbon Appliqué interpretation pictured are on pages 111–116 in my *Romancing Ribbons into Flowers* (EZ/Wright's).

The oil pastel shading, UltraSuede Appliqué, and silk ribbon embroidery of the back cover's Bread and Wine block are taught in the lessons of *Fancy Appliqué*. Whether you are a beginner looking for additional blocks to stretch your skills or someone like me who just can't get enough of Album Appliqué, this book is for you. It comes with my heartfelt thanks and appreciation for your companionship on this joyful journey.

Elly Sienkiewicz
September 2, 1999
Washington, DC

Editor's Note: The Elly Sienkiewicz' Baltimore Beauties Fabric is a designer line from P&B Textiles (1-800-TLC-BEAR). While specific prints referred to in the text may not available at this time, please contact P&B or substitute other fabrics.

PATTERN #3: "Lyre *Scherenschnitte*"*

Type: "Beyond"

To make this block, refer to *Volume I*, Lesson 1 or 2.

Lyres were clearly a favorite Album Quilt motif. They can symbolize All Music in Honor of God, or Divine Music, and thus have intimations of immortality. An ancient instrument, they also reflect the neoclassicism popular in these quilts. I designed this pattern seeing greater potential in one in a "Pennsylvania" Album dated 1848 (from *Forget Me Not*, p. 44). Maxine Satchell, having turned the fine cutwork strings to perfection, suggests how lovely they would look couched in gold thread. Or if you'd like to add the lyre's strings separately, try soutache braid which was sometimes used in the classic Albums.

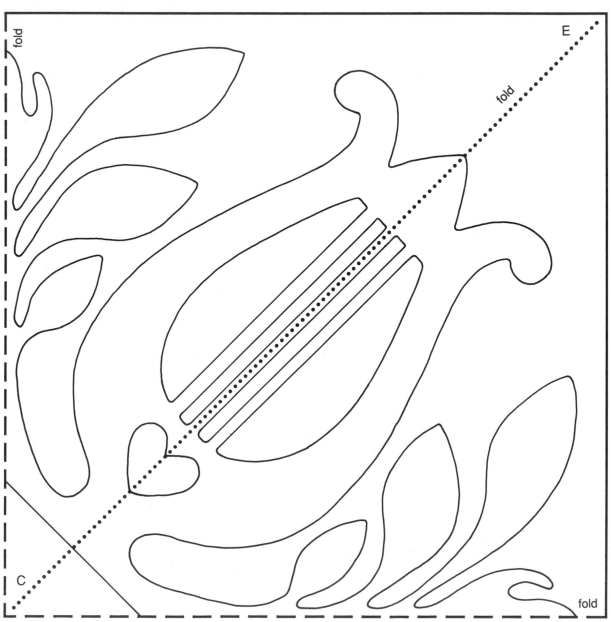

PATTERN #9: "Hearts and Tulips"*

Type: Classic "Baltimore"

To make this block, refer to *Volume I*, Lessons 3 and 5.

Detail: *Volume I*, quilt #6.

This block is so "modern" that it could have been designed today. It seems, however, to have originated in the mid-nineteenth century in the environs of Baltimore. Dramatic in red and green, its symbolic meaning is equally exuberant: tulips suggest a Declaration of Love, and hearts mean Love or Devotion. One could play this possible symbolic intent out a bit further, imputing to the ring of hearts the circle's meaning of Never-ending, or Eternal, Love. Then again, one can't be absolutely sure these are meant to be tulips!

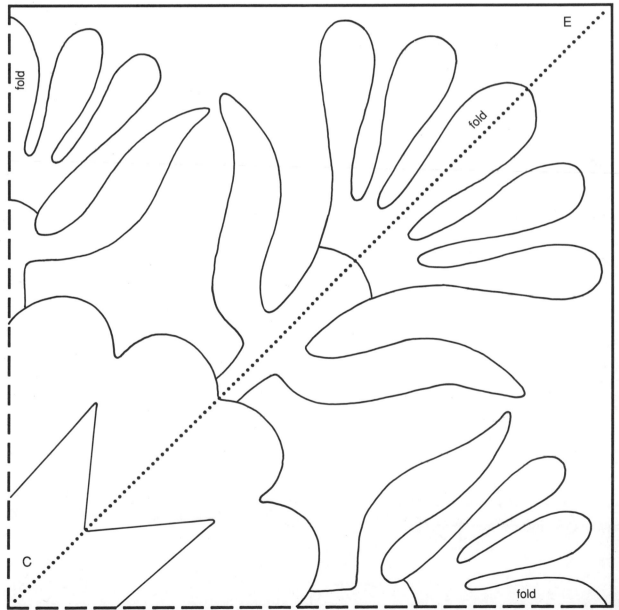

PATTERN #12: "Christmas Cactus I"*

Type: Classic "Baltimore"

To make this block, refer to *Volume I*, Lessons 1 or 2, and 5.

Detail: *Volume I*, quilt #6.

The Christmas cactus seems to have been a relatively oft-repeated block in the classic Album Quilts but this one seems the most graceful, elegant, and realistic.

    The plant, first hybridized in the 1840s by William Buckley, an English gardener, surely seems additional proof that the early Album quiltmakers were very current on their natural history, and took "rational pleasure" in recording the latest botanical imports in their quilts. Not only have their quilts survived, but so have some of these early hybrids as well. "It is not uncommon for a Christmas cactus nurtured in the nineteenth century to survive several generations," writes Judith Hillstrom.

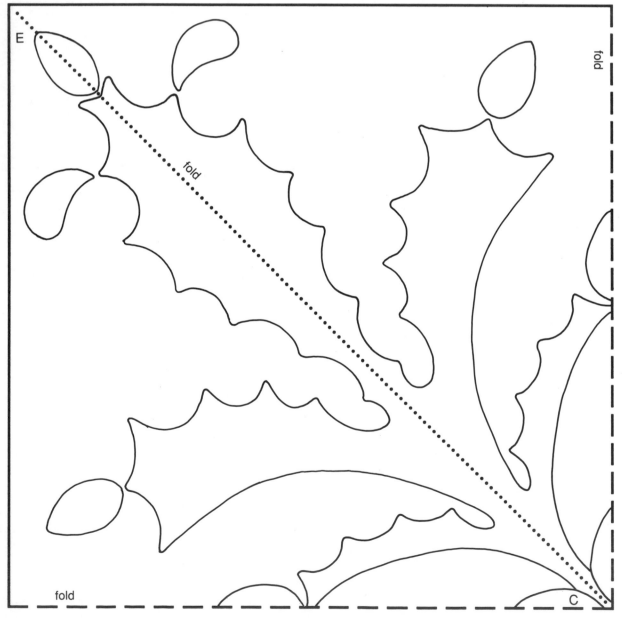

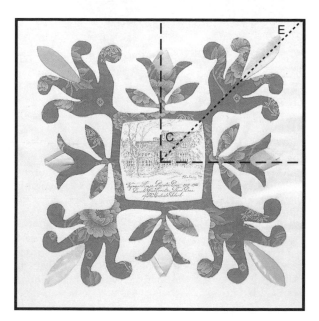

PATTERN #13 "Fleur-de-Lis with Rosebuds III"*

Type: "Beyond"

To make this block, refer to *Volume I*, Lessons 1 or 2, and 6.

This pattern is based on a block from a quilt in the Numsen family. The pattern shows that version although it's been taken a bit "beyond" by the inclusion of folded 3½"-diameter circle rosebuds from Lesson 6. With its bold two-color fleurs-de-lis and enlarged framelike center, it is a particularly graceful and appealing version of the block which recurs in many forms in these classic quilts. Why might this square wreath (symbolizing Earthly Matters), with fleurs-de-lis (see the notes to Pattern #2), and rosebuds (Beauty, Purity, Youth) or as a rose, Love, have been so popular? Was it for its meaning? Did it have a meaning as yet unfathomed? Or did avid pattern collectors simply want the variety of a square wreath added to their Albums?

PATTERN #17: "Rose of Sharon III"*

Type: Classic "Baltimore"

To make this block, refer to *Volume I*, Lessons 1 or 2, 5 or 10.

Detail: *Volume I*, quilt #7.

This particular Rose Wreath I have seen only on mid-nineteenth-century Maryland Album Quilts. Intrigued by its simplicity, I decided to add intricacy to an otherwise plain block so I inked much of it to look like engraving. One flower I left unembellished so you can see the difference the inking has made. See Lessons 3 and 7 (*Volume I*) for instructions on writing and drawing on your block.

I have called this a Rose of Sharon, though others may know it differently. The Rose of Sharon harkens back to its Biblical reference in the Song of Solomon and symbolizes Wedded Love.

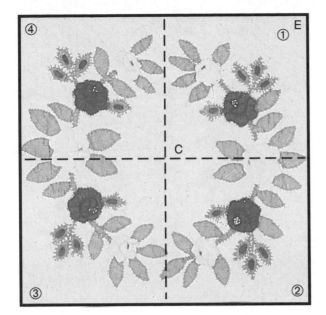

PATTERN #19: "Broken Wreath of Roses"*

Type: Classic "Baltimore"

To make this block, refer to *Volume I*, Lessons 5, 7, 9, or 10.

Another pattern design and construction theme that runs through the classic Baltimore Album Quilts is the stuffed and heavily embroidered one shown by this graceful block. Quite similar is Pattern #20, the "Wreath of Roses." While that is a whole wreath, this is actually a two-half-circle wreath, a rare variation of the more common broken wreath which is broken only at the top. Bright in Victoria green and Turkey red with contrasting white roses, this block entices the quiltmaker who loves the fancywork of embroidered embellishments.

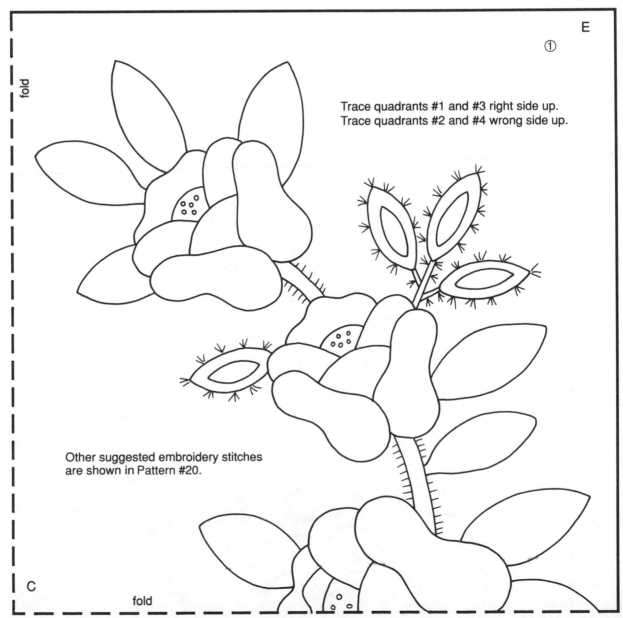

Trace quadrants #1 and #3 right side up.
Trace quadrants #2 and #4 wrong side up.

Other suggested embroidery stitches are shown in Pattern #20.

PATTERN #20: "Wreath of Roses"*

Type: Classic "Baltimore"

To make this block, refer to *Volume I*, Lessons 5, 7, and 9.

Dr. Dunton, recording this quilt in *Old Quilts* (p. 22), provides his usual complete description: "Wreath of Roses. Leaves are of the 3-2 type. (Three outside, two inside between the roses.) Four are white and four red. All are padded and shaded with silk. The wool stitching of the red and white buds and outlining the white roses is light blue. All roses have yellow wool pistils, leaves of black on green of tiny black diamonds (1½ x 3½ mm.) with a small yellow dot in the centre of each. Diamonds are 5 mm. apart diagonally in rows."

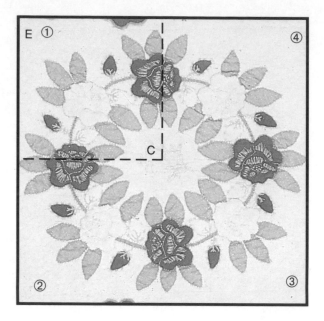

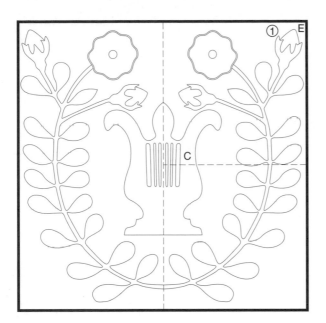

PATTERN #22: "Rose Lyre II"*

Type: Baltimore-style

To make this block, refer to *Volume I*, Lessons 1 or 2, or 5.

Pretty, easy to make, and imbued with sweetly sentimental symbolism, this block may be irresistible. "Sure as the grape grows on the vine/So sure you are my valentine/The rose is red the violet blue/Lilies are fair and so are you."[8] Who does not understand a gift of flowers to be a Token of Affection? From birth, to marriage, to death, we mark the moment with flowers.

Greek and Roman myths tell love stories for almost every kind of flower, but especially for the rose, the symbol of Love. The rose was sacred to Venus, Roman goddess of spring, bloom, and beauty, who was later identified with the Greek Aphrodite as the goddess of love. One myth connects the rose to Cupid, telling that he spilled nectar on

PATTERN #22: "Rose Lyre II"*

Second Page

the ground and it bubbled back up in the form of roses. Explaining nature, as myths do, we are told how the rose got its thorns: Opening only to the kiss of Zephyr, the soft West wind, the rose was kissed one day by amorous Cupid. A bee, trapped inside, stung him. Angry, Venus had Cupid thread the bees on his bowstring: their stings she planted along the stem of the rose where, ever since, they remain as thorns.

All roses mean Love: "And the white rose breathes of love;/O, the red rose is a falcon,/and the white rose is a dove."[9] This love need not be romantic love. And thus we see roses on monument blocks for fallen war heroes.

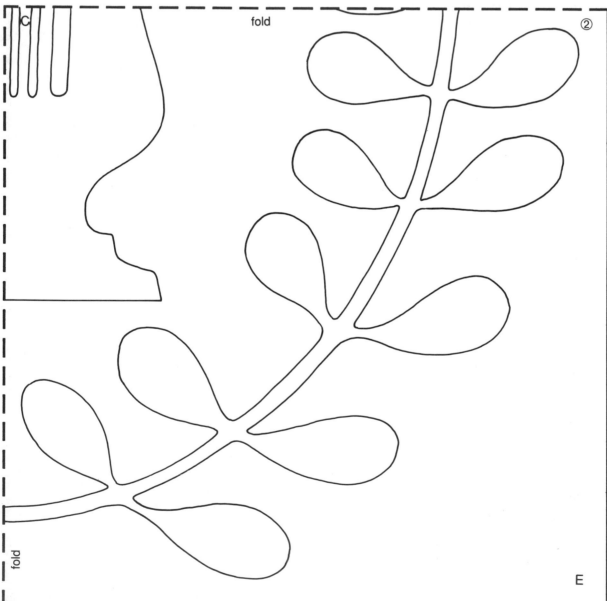

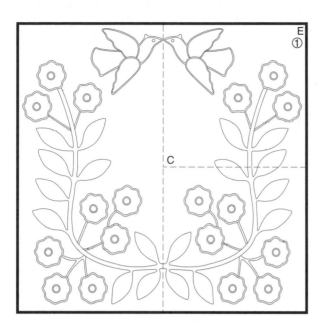

PATTERN #23: "Redbird Lyre"*

Type: Baltimore-style

To make this block, refer to *Volume I*, Lessons 1 or 2, and 5.

Virginia Piland, an extraordinary contemporary quilt-maker, always records on a block if it was sewn on a holiday. This, then is a block to be begun on Valentine's Day, and, drawing heavily on Edna Barth's knowledge,[10] here's why. Perhaps because several species mate in February, Medieval man believed all birds chose their mate on St. Valentine's Day: "For this was on St. Valentine's Day/When every fowl cometh to choose his mate." And, since Noah and the flood, doves had served as messengers, coming in classical times to be connected to Venus and other deities of love. Being of the pigeon family, doves mate for life, are gentle, and murmur comfortingly with their billing and cooing, and so

Note: the lyre stem and leaves are also embroidered in what appears to be button hole or whipped satin stitch.

PATTERN #23: "Redbird Lyre"*

Second Page

prove a happy choice as the bird of love. These doves, on wing above the lyre, which speaks of Divine Music, would seem to sing of Eternal Love. At least, then, we should let them sing of Valentines!

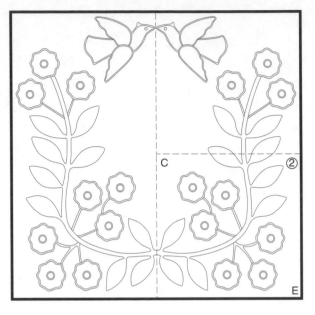

PATTERN #25: "Lyre with Laurel Sprays I"*

Type: Classic "Baltimore"

To make this block, refer to *Volume I*, Lessons 1 or 2, 5, or 10.

Detail: *Volume I*, quilt #4, the classic 1846–47 Baltimore Album Quilt "made for Angeline Hoffman."

This is a particularly successful and endearing version of a simplified lyre block. Lyres are among the most frequently found motifs in these classic quilts. Symbolizing All Music in Honor of God, and Eternal Music, the lyre carries connotations of eternity and things everlasting. Thus, hypothetically, it could mean "in memoriam" in some blocks. Add laurel (for Success, Renown, Victory) to the lyre and this motif might read Eternal Renown, or Victory in Eternity, even Eternal Honor and Devotion. Perhaps the intent was so undeniably good that one did not have to specify!

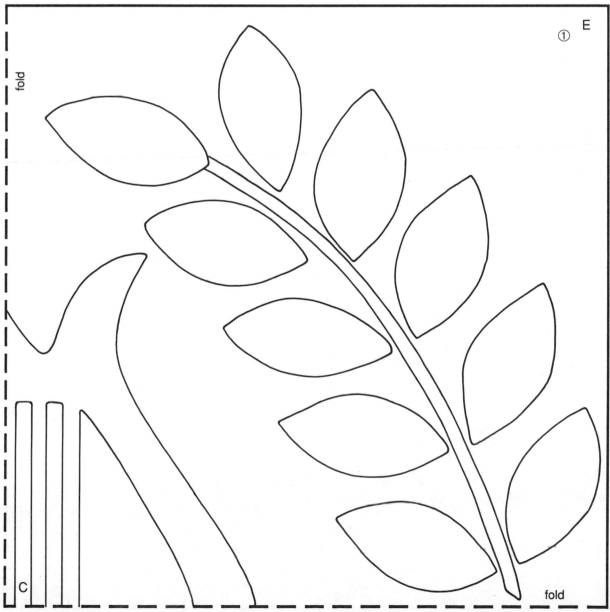

PATTERN #25: "Lyre with Laurel Sprays I"*

Second Page

This heart-decorated lyre seems to be framed by the classic green leaf/red leaf stylization of laurel sprays. Here, though, rather than the red leaves coming at the tips of the sprays, they line one side. All the red on this block could be done by cutwork appliqué (*Volume I*, Lesson 1 or 2); then the green could be added by separate unit appliqué.

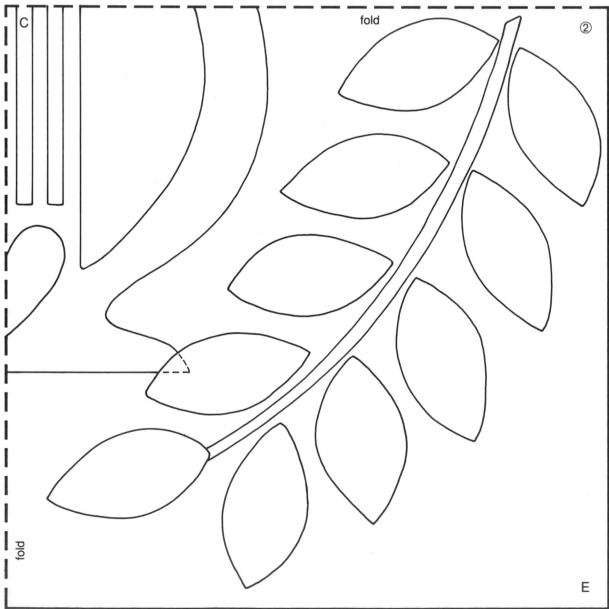

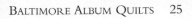

PATTERN #26: "Crossed Sprays of Flowers"*

Type: Classic "Baltimore"

To make this block, refer to *Volume I*, Lessons 1 or 2, 5, or 10.

This is a charming, simple arrangement of a gracefully meandering stem, which, mirrored, supports four stuffed red and yellow tulips, six black-edged red buds, and numerous leaves of varied sizes. Although crossed floral sprays are common in the Album Quilts, this particular version is unusual, perhaps unique. Done by cutwork appliqué, it is relatively quick and easy.

PATTERN #26: "Crossed Sprays of Flowers"*

Second Page

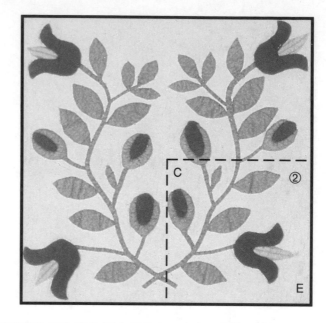

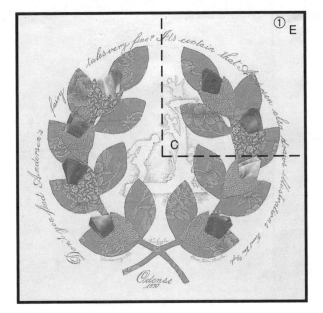

PATTERN #27: "Roses for Hans Christian Andersen"*

Type: "Beyond"

To make this block, refer to *Volume I*, Lessons 1 or 2, and 6.

Who would think this block was quick and easy? Perhaps that's part of its beauty, for the cutwork appliqué leaf/stem framework has been simplified to the utmost with soft outward points and just a few inward points. The folded circle roses are so simple, too, but happily that's your secret! This is an elegant choice to make as a gift, perhaps in a frame to note some special occasion. Or perhaps your gift will be to a Friendship Album in classic Baltimore tradition.

PATTERN #27: "Roses for Hans Christian Andersen"*

Second Page

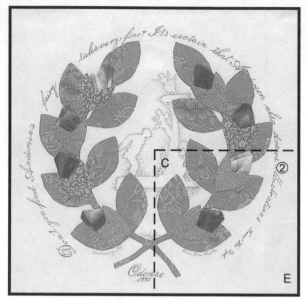

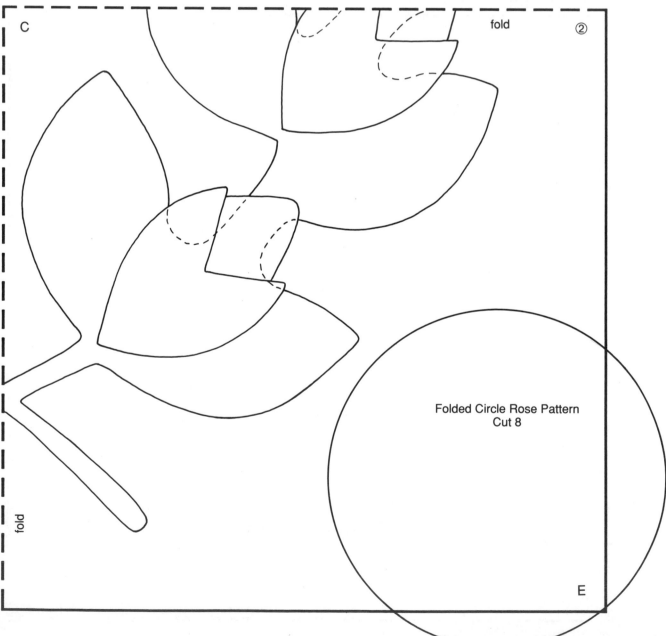

C

fold

②

fold

Folded Circle Rose Pattern
Cut 8

E

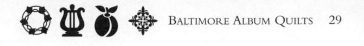

PATTERN #28: "Grapevine Lyre Wreath"*

Type: "Beyond"

To make this block, refer to *Volume I*, Lesson 9 or 10.

Framing a Hans Christian Andersen papercut in silhouette, this is another of my designs from the Odense Album Quilt.

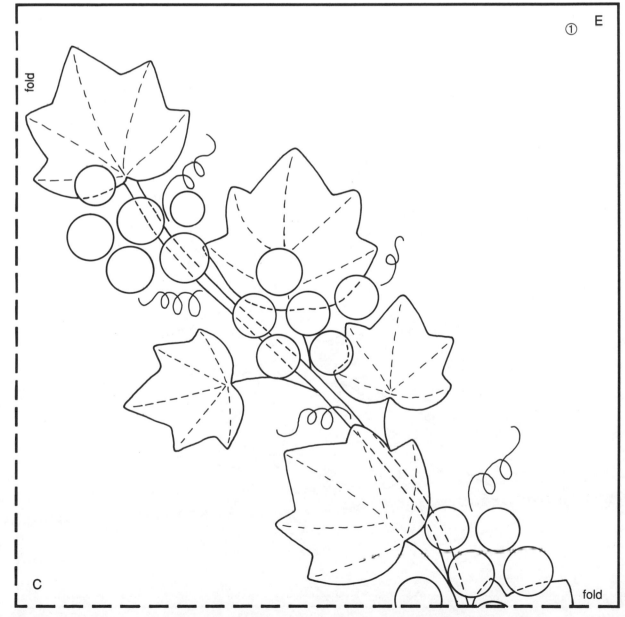

PATTERN #28: "Grapevine Lyre Wreath"*

Second Page

PATTERN #29: "Vase of Full-Blown Roses IV"*

Type: Classic "Baltimore"

To make this block, refer to *Volume I*, Lessons 5, 9, or 10.

The vase of full-blown roses was often repeated in delightful variety. The combination of three red and one white rose seems to have been a favorite, whether for aesthetic or symbolic reasons. The language of flowers offers little information on that score, except to suggest that a white rose means Purity or "I am worthy of you." A vase of full-blown roses means a Token of Gratitude. Elegantly embroidered, this block is a needlework gem. The vase is top-stitched in the clamshell pattern. To date, it seems to be a one-of-a-kind rendition of this block, placed in a position of pride and honor at the center of the quilt.

PATTERN #29: "Vase of Full-Blown Roses IV"*

Second Page

fold

②

Buds and
vase handles have
white wool or cotton
whip stitch overcasting
one or more edges.

C

fold

E

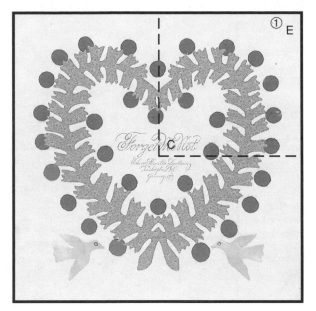

PATTERN #31: "Cherry Wreath with Bluebirds I and II"*

Type: Classic "Baltimore"

To make this block, refer to *Volume I*, Lessons 1 or 2, 5, and 9.

Wreathed hearts are among the most often repeated of the classic Album Quilt blocks. There are variations in both the style of the vine-wreathed hearts and in the motifs which sometimes accompany them; crossed keys (Keys to the Heart, Love), birds (Life of the Soul), kissing "lovebirds" (actually small parrots), hearts paired (True Love), and arrow-pierced hearts (Lovestruck or Repentance) are among these. Vine-wreathed hearts are both beautiful and imbued with symbolic meaning. Hearts mean Love, Devotion, Charity, or, to Scandinavians, Good Luck. The vine, if a grapevine, carries the meaning for Christians of the Church.

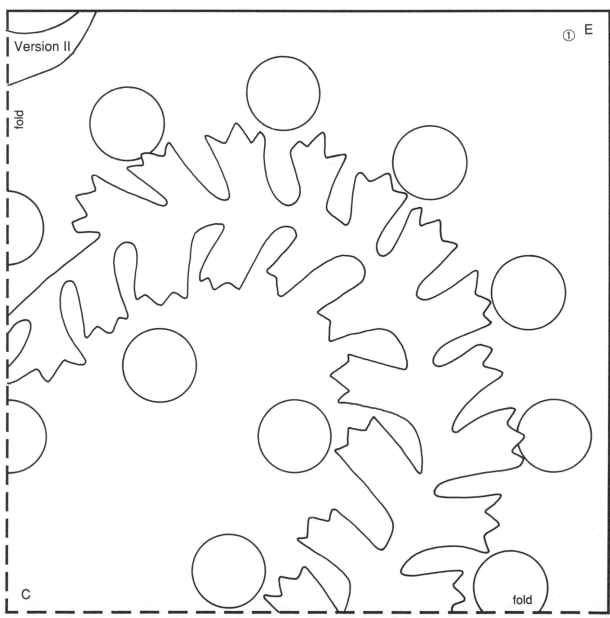

PATTERN #31: "Cherry Wreath with Bluebirds I and II"*

Second Page

Version II

For Version II, place the centerfold of the heart on the diagonal centerfold of the fabric.

Friendships Offering

Version I

Forget Me Not

C

fold

fold

②

E

PATTERN #32: "Diagonal Floral Spray I"*
(Shown with Pattern #33)

Type: Classic "Baltimore"

To make this block, refer to *Volume I*, Lessons 1 or 2, 5, and 9. See also Appendix I in this book.

Of course, one cannot prove beyond a doubt if a specific flower was intended in this block's prototype. However, these flowers look very much like peonies. Another version of the peony may be seen as the central medallion and border motif in quilts #7 and #8 in *Volume I*. Referring to our floral vocabulary, the peony symbolizes Healing and is thus a benevolent symbol to include in an Album Quilt.

These diagonal sprays occur with some frequency in the Baltimore Album Quilts. It occurred to me that this

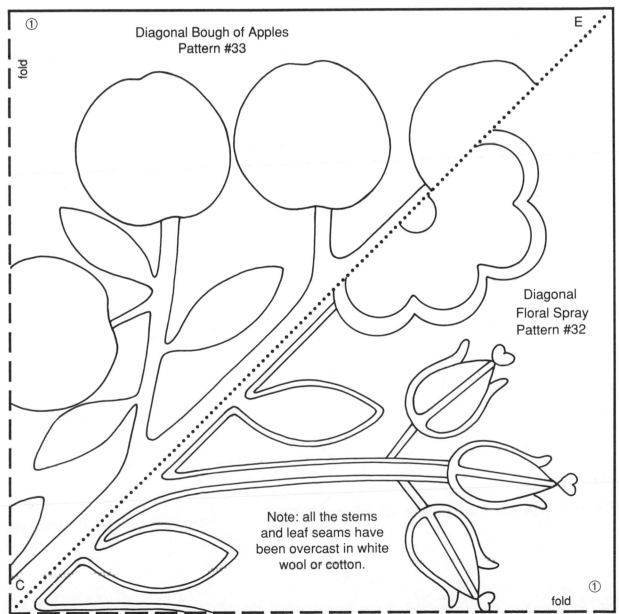

Diagonal Bough of Apples
Pattern #33

Diagonal
Floral Spray
Pattern #32

Note: all the stems
and leaf seams have
been overcast in white
wool or cotton.

fold

PATTERN #32: "Diagonal Floral Spray I"*

Second Page

diagonal design would be particularly effective pointing inward from the four corners of a quilt. It should be simple enough for those wanting multiple versions of this design to substitute alternate blooms on these stems. Undoubtedly the original of this block was done by separate unit appliqué with discrete stems, leaves, and flowers. It is so easily done by cutwork appliqué that our pattern is drafted for that method. The blooms appear to be padded and the maker has made the block quite elegant by extensive embroidery, probably in wool. In the interests of saving space, the spray of roses (Pattern #32) is shown on the right-hand diagonal half of this four-page pattern, the apple bough (Pattern #33) on the left-hand side.

This embroidery line is drawn on quadrant #1 only. If you'd prefer not to do all those embellishing stitches, the leaves and stems have been drawn for cutaway appliqué.

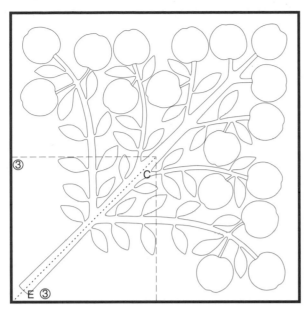

PATTERN #33: "Diagonal Bough of Apples"*
(Shown with Pattern #32)

Third Page

Type: Baltimore-style

To make this block, refer to *Volume I*, Lessons 1 or 2, 5, or 10.

Apples recur in the classic Baltimore Album Quilts. In the most ornate blocks, they nest in baskets or tumble out of cornucopias. In simpler blocks, they come in wreaths. This laden apple branch is a much rarer depiction of the fruit. A look at its symbolism shows a significantly different meaning for a bough of apples as opposed to apples in general. A single apple symbolizes Perpetual Concord, and Salvation when depicted in Christ's hands (or temptation in Adam's hands). But an apple bough harkens back to Greek mythology,

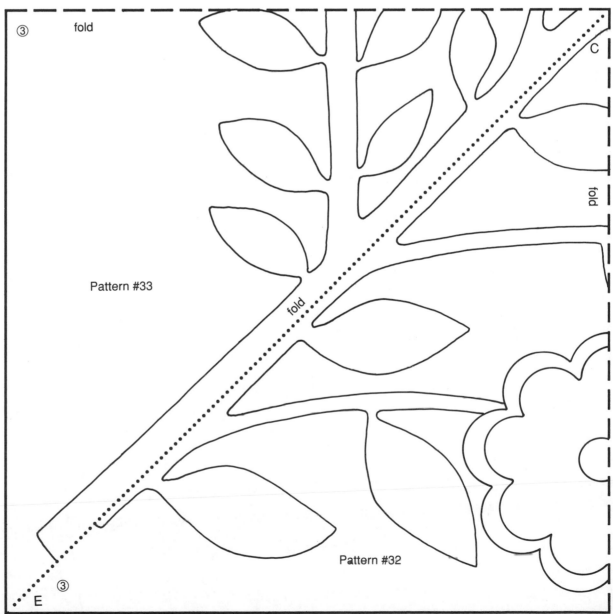

Pattern #33

Pattern #32

PATTERN #33: "Diagonal Bough of Apples"*

Fourth Page

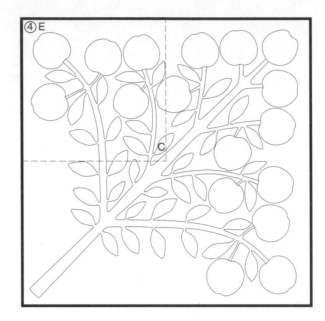

signifying Transport to Elysium where, the dictionary reminds us, the Elysian Fields are located. Hence Elysian as an adjective means 'happy, blissful, delightful.' The Elysian Fields were where virtuous people went after death, a concept which translated in Chrisitanity to Heaven. Elysium is any place or condition of ideal bliss or complete happiness. Hardly disputable intents for an Album quilt!

Going back even further to ancient Hebraic times, Love and Fertility are symbolized by the apple. Barth tells us that Hebrew women who wanted to bear a child mixed the sap of an apple tree with their bathwater, and that Norse gods ate apples to attain perpetual youth. Could that possibly have evolved into the familiar "An apple a day keeps the doctor away"? For my appliqué time, I'd sooner invest in the Elysian field theory!

PATTERN #34: "Folk Art Vase of Flowers"*
(Shown with Pattern #35)

Type: Classic "Baltimore"

To make this block, refer to *Volume I*, Lessons 1 or 2, 5, or 10.

This is a brightly beautiful diagonally set vase of flowers. If you're looking for blocks which can point in towards the center of your quilt, this is one of only a handful of possibilities. Dr. Dunton notes (in *Old Quilts*, p. 27) that "the base of the vase is of the shaded [rainbow fabric] blue, but a very narrow portion at the bottom is tan, indicating that these shaded blues were cut from a striped fabric."

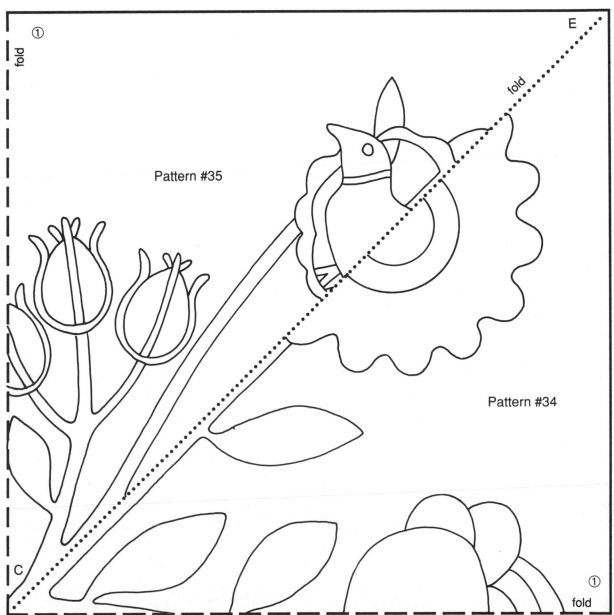

PATTERN #34: "Folk Art Vase of Flowers"*

Second Page

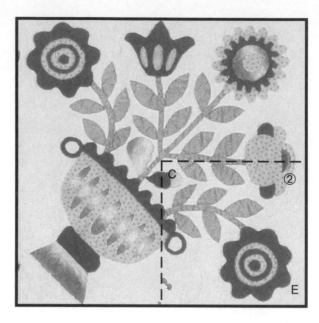

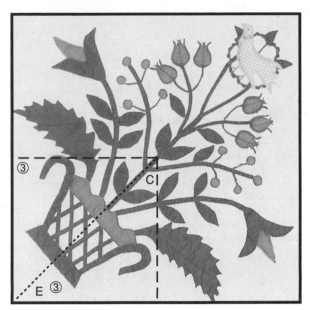

PATTERN #35: "Bird Bedecked Bouquet"*
(Shown with Pattern #34)

Third Page

Type: Baltimore-style

To make this block, refer to *Volume I*, Lessons 1, 5, 9, or 10.

Charming, and not overly difficult, this block would seem to wish for babies. Filled with buds, a bird on a nest (as yet empty), and cherries (for Sweet Character?), this block seems destined for a Bride's Quilt. The block's maker would seem to be giving her blessing upon what she hopes will be a fruitful union.

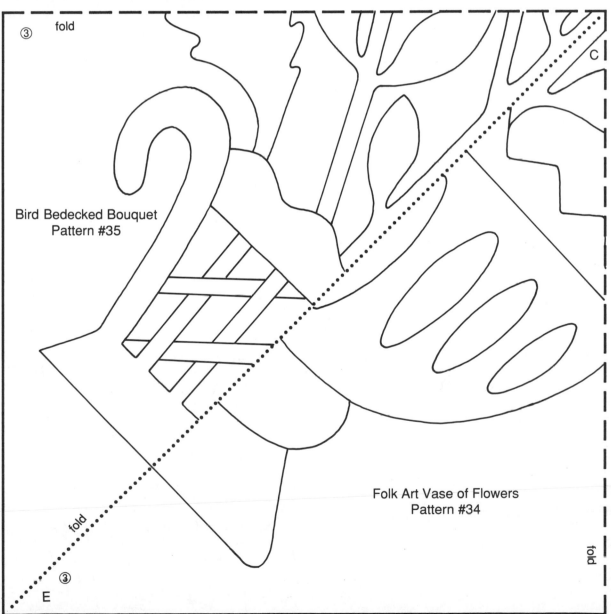

Bird Bedecked Bouquet
Pattern #35

Folk Art Vase of Flowers
Pattern #34

PATTERN #35: "Bird Bedecked Bouquet"*

Fourth Page

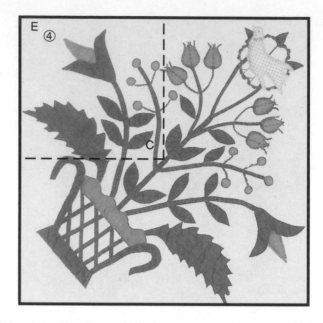

E ④

A.

Template A for the
left stem bloom
opposite B on Pattern #34.

fold

fold

C

fold

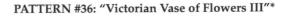

PATTERN #36: "Victorian Vase of Flowers III"*

Type: Classic "Baltimore"

To make this block, refer to *Volume I*, Lessons 5, 9, or 10. See also Appendix I in this book.

Many who dream of Album Quilts, dream of such a block, for this sort of ornate, realistic, Victorian block is one of the characteristic styles of the classic Baltimore Album Quilts. Today's needleartist will observe that the contours of this neoclassic vase have been cleverly depicted by a sophisticated rainbow print which suggests its three-dimensional quality. The print usage progresses upward in a delightful mixture of subtly shaded prints and solids, small calico-like prints, and cut-out motifs to show leaves and flowers. That print of a brown circle forming the center of the blue flowers is one familiar to us in these quilts, as is the convention of splitting fruits

PATTERN #36: "Victorian Vase of Flowers III"*

Second Page

and depicting a bird's eye with a flower. She will have admired (and possibly by now have herself done some of) the inking of moss rose hairs, stems, and leaf veins. Today's quiltmaker will be intrigued by the variety of floral forms and may wonder if this is a particularly original rendition of the three red, one white full-blown rose theme. (See the notes for Pattern #29.)

But what if you were the Victorian quiltmaker who designed this or so many similar blocks of vases and flowers? Might you intend this to be an urn, a footed or pedestaled vase? Long used to hold the ashes of the dead after cremation, the urn can figuratively imply the Grave; flowers, the Soul Heaven Bound; and the bird signifying Life of the Soul, promising immortality in Resurrection. Or, if a dove, symbolizing Innocence, the Holy Spirit, and, again, bearing the message of salvation.

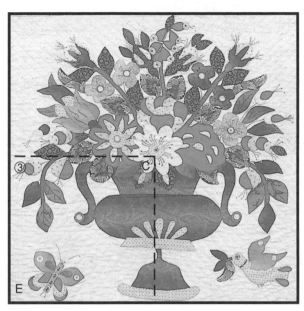

PATTERN #36: "Victorian Vase of Flowers III"*

Third Page

If you lived in mid-nineteenth-century Baltimore, as this block's maker surely must have, your design vocabulary would be permeated by the symbolism of fraternal orders; an urn of flowers would seem the perfect mode for depicting the pot of incense, for indeed it was at times so depicted in Masonic renderings. You would know that the pot of incense is the emblem of a pure heart, "which is always an acceptable sacrifice to the Deity; and, as this glows with fervent heat, so should our hearts continually glow with gratitude to the great beneficent Author of our existence, for the manifold blessings and comforts we enjoy." And, had you been a Daughter of Rebekah, you would know to present this symbol a bit differently, still, perhaps as an urn of flowers, but that pot of incense would be shown sitting upon the altar, even on a simple slab, for burning incense. And why

PATTERN #36: "Victorian Vase of Flowers III"*

Fourth Page

would you not note that this was what you were depicting? Ah, yes, quite right. How silly of me to ask. Everybody does know it.

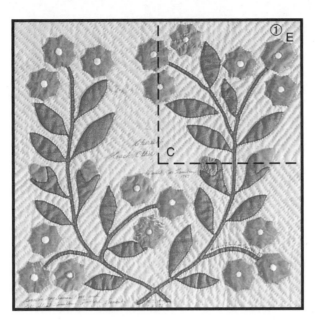

PATTERN #37: "Asymmetrical Spray of Red Blossoms I"*

Type: Classic "Baltimore"

To make this block, refer to *Volume I*, Lessons 1 or 2, and 5.

Detail: *Volume I*, quilt #6.

This arrangement of these unnamed flowers is repeated over and over in the classic Baltimore Album Quilts, with only slight variations. Gracefully balanced in asymmetry, an aesthetic quality much sought after by the makers of these classic quilts, one can understand why the block was so well-loved. And speaking of love, if I had to guess, I'd say, both from the flower and the frequency with which it is portrayed, that we are looking at a rosebush.

I approached this block by doing the green as one piece by cutwork appliqué. The flowers I did by needle-turn, and reverse appliquéd or buttonholed most of the centers. A few centers I did over a plastic template cut by

PATTERN #37: "Asymmetrical Spray of Red Blossoms I"*

Second Page

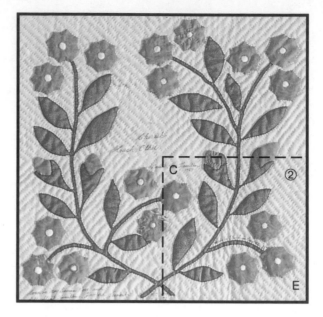

a paper punch using the methods described in Lesson 9 (*Volume I*). Possibly you can recognize these for their more precise circular shape.

I can't resist concluding this botannical conjecture with a quote reported in *The Heyday of Natural History* (p. 114) which cuts periously close to needlewomen, including the quiltmakers of today as well as of yesterday. In addition, it reminds us of the quantity of publications available on botanical themes in the 1840s and 1850s. "Charles Kingsley reported patronizingly at the height of the [fern collecting] craze that it was having an entirely beneficial effect on the nation's womenfolk: Your daughters, perhaps, have been seized with the prevailing 'Pteridomania,' wrangling over unpronounceable names of species (which seem to be different in each new fern book they buy) till Pteridomania seems to you somewhat

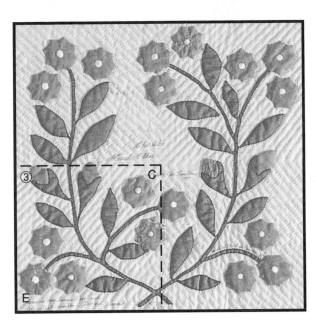

PATTERN #37: "Asymmetrical Spray of Red Blossoms I"*

Third Page

of a bore: and yet you cannot deny that they find an enjoyment in it, and are more active, more cheerful, more self-forgetful over it, than they would have been over novels and gossips, crochet and Berlin-wool. At least you will confess that the abomination of 'Fancy work,' that standing cloak for dreamy idleness, has all but vanished from your drawing-room since the 'Lady-ferns' and 'Venus's hair' appeared."

PATTERN #37: "Asymmetrical Spray of Red Blossoms I"*

Fourth Page

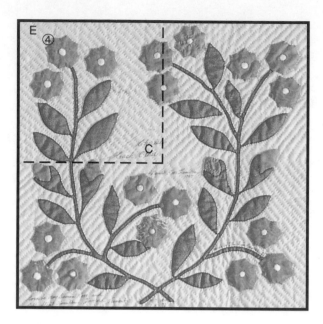

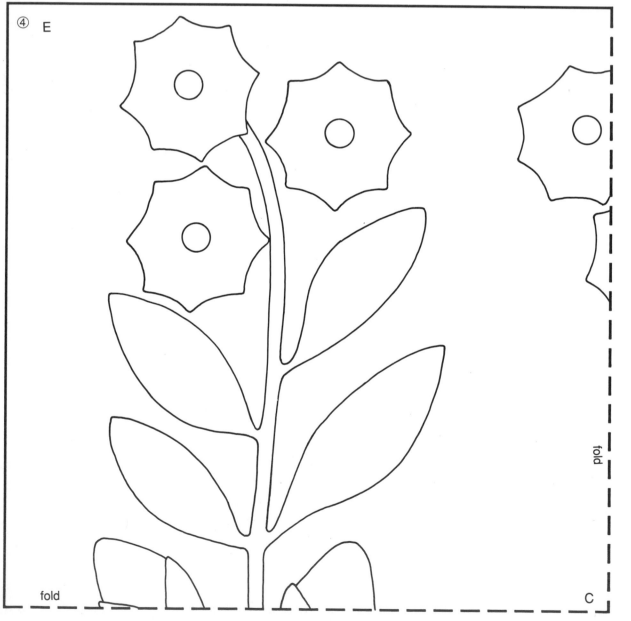

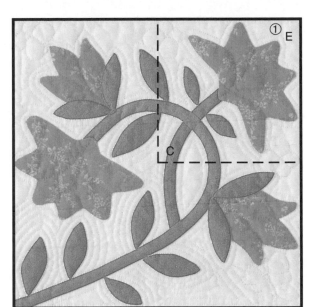

PATTERN #38: "Peony Medallion Center"*

Type: Possibly "Beyond"

To make this block, refer to *Volume I*, Lessons 5, 9, and 10.

Detail: *Volume I*, quilt #7.

One of the significant aspects of the classic quilts, discussed in *Volume II*, is the various sets of the Baltimore Album Quilts. While the twenty-five-block set (5 x 5) seems the most typical (and has a clear center), there are many quilts in a sixteen-block set which, being even numbered, do not have a center block. Many of the classic quilts' makers seem to have tried to organize the Album's blocks and to create an internal design, often with a focus on the center.

PATTERN #38: "Peony Medallion Center"*

Second Page

I have called this pattern's flower the "peony," for so it appears to me. Moreover, peonies have the pleasing symbolism of Healing. In the original quilt,[14] the same repeat block center medallion is in a thirty-six-block quilt. It forms the center of quilt #8 (*Volume I*) with thirty-six blocks, and of quilt #7, with sixteen blocks. One other quilt, a classic Baltimore Album, displays this same style of a four-repeat block center. But in that quilt, it is sixteen large strawberries that form the quilt's medallion center focus. To get this peony block pattern to face both left and right, trace the pattern onto a 12½"-square sheet of paper, then trace the reverse of it on a lightbox. The two patterns form the four blocks used for the central medallion.

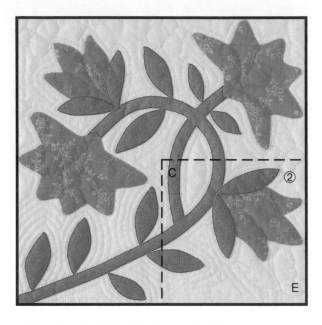

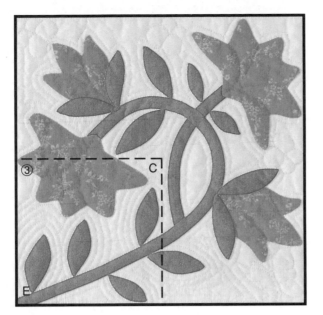

PATTERN #38: "Peony Medallion Center"*

Third Page

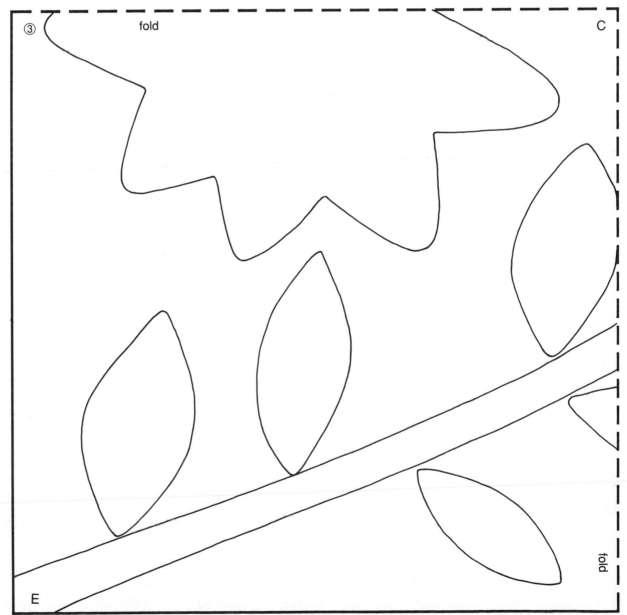

PATTERN #38: "Peony Medallion Center"*

Fourth Page

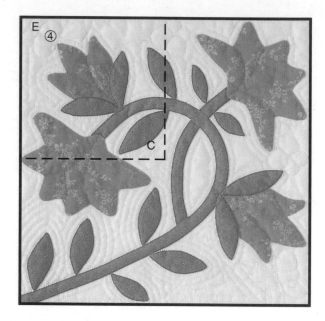

PATTERN #39: "Albertine's Rose Climber"*

Type: "Beyond"

To make this block, refer to *Volume I*, Lessons 1 or 2, 5, and 10.

Detail: *Volume I*, quilt #7.

This block is an original design by Albertine Veenstra. Appearing in two slightly varied versions in quilt #7 (*Volume I*), it's one of the blocks for which people seem most to want a pattern. This version is based on Albertine's design. Her roses are done in a glossy sateen and are embellished with skillfully embroidered stem, outline, or crewel stitch (they are essentially all the same stitch). This pattern shows a layered rose, another design possibility.

PATTERN #39: "Albertine's Rose Climber"*

Second Page

PATTERN #39: "Albertine's Rose Climber"*

Third Page

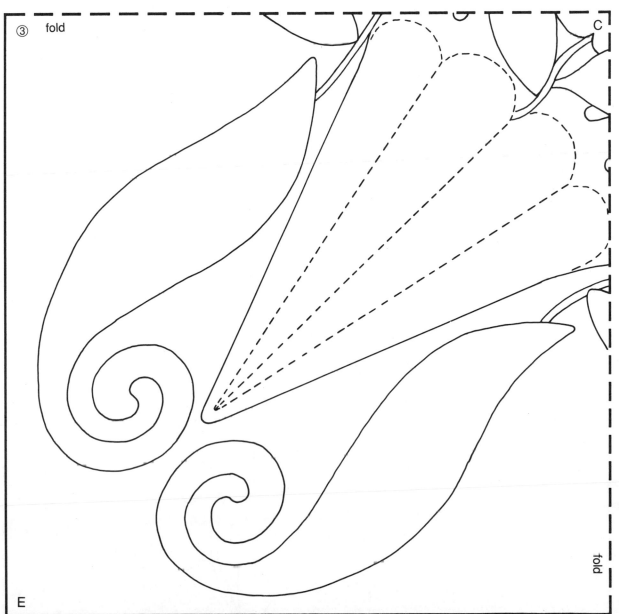

PATTERN #39: "Albertine's Rose Climber"*

Fourth Page

PATTERN #41: "Victorian Basket of Flowers IV"*

Type: Classic "Baltimore"

To make this block, refer to *Volume I*, Lessons 5, 9, or 10.

Detail: *Volume I*, quilt #2.

Ornate, realistic, Victorian, a woven basket—and yet not overwhelming at that. This basket, with a bit of ruffled trim at the bottom, is a style repeated in an exquisite Album Quilt belonging to the Smithsonian Institution in Washington.

PATTERN #41: "Victorian Basket of Flowers IV"*

Second Page

PATTERN #41: "Victorian Basket of Flowers IV"*

Third Page

PATTERN #41: "Victorian Basket of Flowers IV"*

Fourth Page

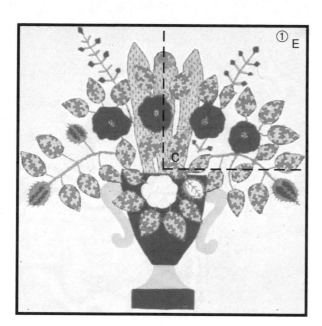

PATTERN #43: "Victorian Vase of Flowers I"*

Type: Classic "Baltimore"

To make this block, refer to *Volume I*, Lessons 5, 9, or 10.

A most endearing neoclassical vase of flowers, this appears to be one of a kind. It is a bit smaller than the other blocks in its quilt and it is so depicted here. The appliqué is quite straightforward, and moderately time-consuming. But the embroidery, which really makes this block visually, will also make it take considerably longer to do.

PATTERN #43: "Victorian Vase of Flowers I"*

Second Page

PATTERN #45: "Melodies of Love"*

Type: Classic "Baltimore"

To make this block, refer to *Volume I*, Lesson(s) 5, 9, or 10.

Detail: *Volume I*, quilt #2.

Love and music—oh, sweet harmony!—would seem to be the theme here. The block appears to have both romantic and neoclassical overtones, with a heart, sealed epistle, music, and arrows symbolizing Romantic Love through the god Eros amid fronds of graceful flowers. Despite the visual appeal of this pattern, I've only seen two other blocks, all three slightly different, which depict it. This sort of decorative motif might be expected to be familiar to the Baltimore Albums' makers from printed textiles in vogue at the time. That decorative arts source might in itself explain this complex and not often repeated design.

PATTERN #45: "Melodies of Love"*

Second Page

This music block might be a reference to one or more of the German social clubs, many of which emphasized musical themes as a basis for fraternizing. Close to 200,000 German immigrants entered through the Port of Baltimore in the three decades before the Civil War. Some took off to settle the Midwest but a sizeable number stayed in Baltimore. The Germans who had come earlier had farmed the frontier and turned Baltimore into a major grain port. By midcentury, they had been virtually assimilated.

Many of the newer German immigrants prospered in the tobacco export trade, but with a few notable exceptions they were regarded as foreigners. They faced a formidable language barrier and, on top of this, they seemed to prefer their own kind and their own customs. What developed was a social system consisting of an "elaborate organization of clubs, each catering to a

PATTERN #45: "Melodies of Love"*

Third Page

different class. At the top of the pile was the Germania Club which was founded in 1840. It was the most exclusive of all and its membership was confined to the wealthy merchants.... Next to the Germania in social importance was the Concordia, founded in 1847. This club emphasized a literary and musical program that appealed to the intellectuals of the upper middle class. Its musical and dramatic divisions sponsored ambitious productions that gave it unusual distinctions. A cut below the Germania and the Concordia were the singing societies. The oldest of these was the Liederkranz which was organized in 1836 out of the choir of Zion Church.... Other singing societies stemming from choirs and catering to a lower social group were the Harmonie and the Arion. On the other hand, the German Mannechor, founded in 1856, was reserved primarily for the families of the wealthy merchants. These various singing societies

PATTERN #45: "Melodies of Love"*

Fourth Page

met annually with similar societies in Philadelphia and other cities for a national sangerfest. At the bottom of the social scale were the gymnastic clubs. These appealed to the rank and file of immigrants and were part of the Turner movement whose basic concept was a healthy mind in a healthy body."

There is also a musical instrument of some sort in the central block (*Volume I*, quilt #2 in the Color Section) in which this pattern I've dubbed "Melodies of Love" appears. The musical instrument, seemingly symbolic, appears with our national emblem, the eagle (Courage, Generosity, Highest Inspiration, Resurrection) in whose talons the bundle of arrows signifies Unity. The other leg's talons clasp a branch of laurel (Triumph, Victory, Eternity) and the Phrygian cap, symbol of freedom from slavery.

PATTERN #46: "The Album"*

Type: Classic "Baltimore"

To make this block, refer to *Volume I*, Lesson 7, 5, 9, and 10.

Detail: *Volume I*, quilt #2.

"The Album" seems increasingly to inform our sense of these quilts, for as all albums are collections upon a theme, so, too, are Album Quilts. The themes of these Album Quilts seem to vary widely and many remain elusive. A favorite Album block in the ornate, realistic, Victorian style, is the bird holding a book above flowers: flowers in a basket, or, as here, in a wreath. The books are commonly labeled, for which we are grateful! Some are marked Bible, others Sacred Melodies, some Album, some have a person s name inscribed on them, and most seem to have a ribbon in them marking a

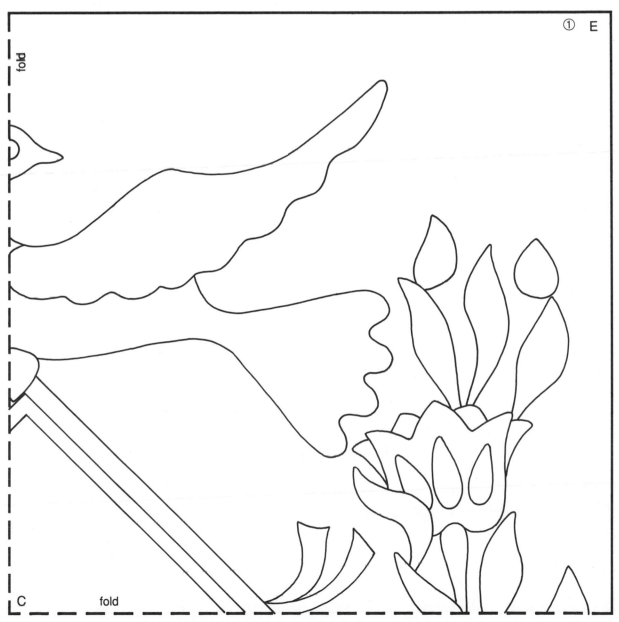

PATTERN #46: "The Album"*

Second Page

page. This elegant block is complex, yet approachable, and would make a wonderful addition to any of our Albums!

PATTERN #46: "The Album"*

Third Page

PATTERN #46: "The Album"*

Fourth Page

PATTERN #47: *"Bouquet avec Trois Oiseaux"**

Type: Classic "Baltimore"

To make this block, refer to *Volume I*, Lessons 5, 7, 9, or 10.

An exquisite block, but why the French? To help gain understanding of these quilts, I have been studying autograph and other albums of the 1840s through the 1870s. One, an 1870s autograph album in the manuscript collection of the Winterthur Museum, is replete with calligraphy, poems, sketches, inscriptions from as far apart as New York and Atlanta, and some French! One person addresses the album's owner, *Ma chère Camille* (my dear Camille) and closes, *Votre vieille Amie* (your old friend), with a careful paragraph of French in between. It is all very intriguing. Was Camille

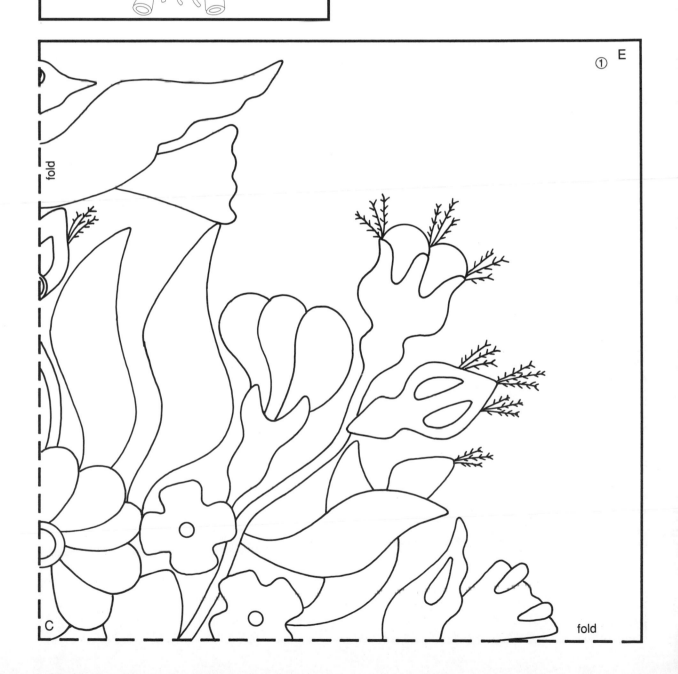

PATTERN #47: *"Bouquet avec Trois Oiseaux"**

Second Page

French? Were these schoolgirls who had all learned French together? More mysteries, and this time compounded by a foreign tongue!

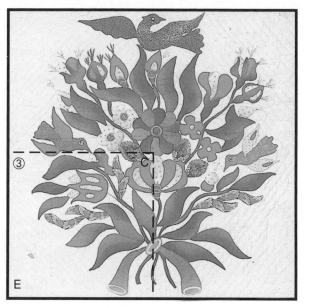

PATTERN #47: *"Bouquet avec Trois Oiseaux"**

Third Page

PATTERN #47: *"Bouquet avec Trois Oiseaux"**

Fourth Page

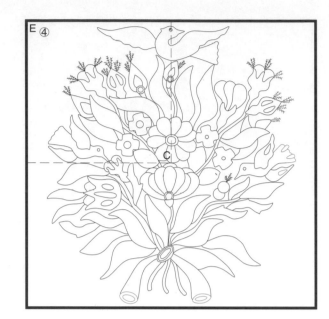

PATTERN #48: "Lyre with Wreath, Bird, and Crown"*

Type: Classic "Baltimore"

To make this block, refer to *Volume I*, Lessons 5, 7, 9, or 10.

This perfectly beautiful block seems imbued with symbolic intent. The instrument here seems to be not a lyre, but a harp, perhaps the Sacred Harp, the emblem of All Music in Honor of God. An ancient instrument, the harp goes back to the Mesopotamian cradle of civilization and to ancient Egypt. In Norse mythology, the harp was the emblem of a ladder between Earth and Heaven and heroes asked to be buried with it, for that reason. This harp, with its intimations of immortality, would seem to have a hero's crown left on it. The language of flowers tells us that a crown of wild olive is a symbol of Victory, as is a crown of laurel. One could surmise that this crown

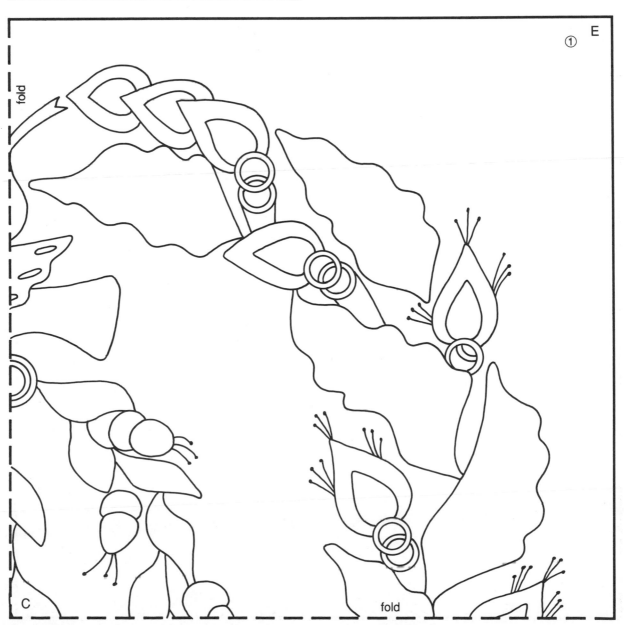

PATTERN #48: "Lyre with Wreath, Bird, and Crown"*

Second Page

might be wild olive, for it is also the sprig in the dove's beak in block D-2 in this quilt. The bird, as a dove, is God's messenger, and stands for Life of the Soul. Exquisite, this block's message is well-clouded by time, but would seem to refer to the fallen heroes represented by the monuments.

Live oak, native to Texas and a symbol on the Texas state seal, seems represented by the outer wreath. If so, this block could honor the fallen Mexican War heroes, Ringgold, Watson, or all. Passionately, through without a word, it echoes the injunction engraved on an adobe wall at the Alamo: "Be silent, friend, here heroes died, to blaze a trail, for other men." In silence, then, this lovely quilt ties present heroes to past. It links Baltimoreans to the nation's service, from Baltimore Harbor to Texas, from the early century to midpoint.

PATTERN #48: "Lyre with Wreath, Bird, and Crown"*

Third Page

Again, a starlike yellow embroidery atop the monument in one Album Quilt might be the same Masonic compass and square symbol marking the plaque at the Alamo which reads: "Honoring these masons, James Bonham, James Bowie, David Crockett, Almaron Dickerson, William Barrett Travis, and those unidentified masons who gave their lives in the Battle of the Alamo, March 6, 1836"

This block motif is repeated elsewhere in the Baltimore Albums and as with most repeated blocks, the pattern or its placement on the block varies a bit from one quilt to another. To prove the point, and to enrich our offering, you are shown in one block, and the pattern is drafted from a second block. The bird in the latter is different and the wreath a bit fuller. Yet the fabrics in each block seem similar, and the shapes so

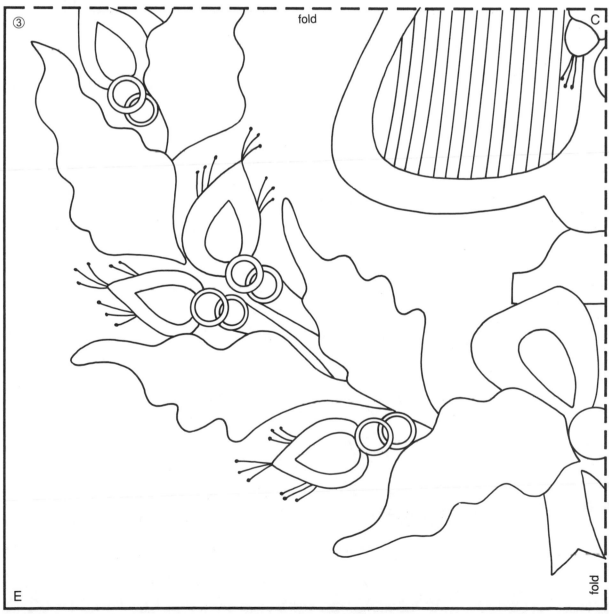

PATTERN #48: "Lyre with Wreath, Bird, and Crown"*

Fourth Page

close that one has the impression two different patterns were drawn by two different people on the same theme or from the same picture.

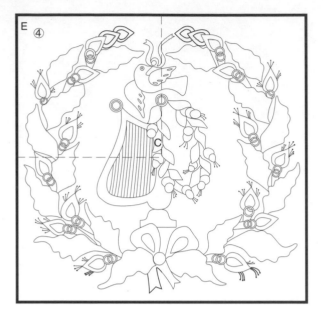

PATTERN #49: "Cornucopia II"*

Type: Classic "Baltimore"

To make this block, refer to *Volume I*, Lessons 5, 7, or 10.

Detail: *Volume I*, quilt #2.

Cornucopias occur frequently in the classic Baltimore Album Quilts. Sometimes they are shown diagonally on the block and make wonderful corner blocks, offering their plenty towards the quilt's center (see *Spoken Without a Word*, p. 60). Sometimes they are filled with fruits, sometimes flowers, sometimes both. And sometimes they appear with acorns thrown in to symbolize Longevity and Immortality. The one patterned here is a particularly beautiful block with the balancing design elements of a fruit and a bird to the left and right of the tip. These square the block off so that it fits in well with other blocks

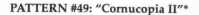

PATTERN #49: "Cornucopia II"*

Second Page

which are set straight. It fills the block in a similar fashion to upright bouquets and vases of flowers.

Beyond being a lovely neoclassical design motif, the cornucopia was an important Odd Fellow symbol. This at a time when fraternal orders were immensely popular, so much so that many people belonged to several at once. Odd Fellowdom, in the United States, started with Lodge #1 being built in Baltimore in 1819. Possibly most importantly, a women's degree of Odd Fellowdom, the Daughters of Rebekah, was founded in 1851 in Baltimore. Great excitement, meetings in homes, and conceivably fundraising, which may have included the making of quilt blocks, and quilts for sale, preceded the building and dedication of the Crown Rebekah Lodge #1 in Baltimore on Fels Road.

The issue of fraternal symbolism is dealt with in more detail in *Volume II*, but suffice it to say that certain block

PATTERN #49: "Cornucopia II"*

Third Page

motifs that we think of as classic Album Quilt blocks in the uniquely ornate, realistic, Victorian style, designs which include cornucopias and doves bearing an olive branch within an elaborate wreath, are Odd Fellow/ Rebekah symbols and may have been being used intentionally as such.

A second reason why cornucopias may have held the limelight is pointed out by Edna Barth. Though we grew up on tales of the Pilgrims' famous harvest feast of 1621, few of us are aware that Thanksgiving did not become a national holiday until centuries later. Mrs. Sarah Josepha Hale, editor of the magazine *Godey's Lady's Book*, and probably well-known by name at least to many makers of the Baltimore-area Album Quilts, felt that a day of Thanksgiving should be celebrated by the whole nation at one time. For twenty years she urged this through her articles, letters to presidents and governors,

③ fold   C

E   fold

PATTERN #49: "Cornucopia II"*

Fourth Page

and her speeches. Like the Album Quilts' makers, Mrs. Hale could feel the chill winds of the Civil War approaching and she apparently believed a national Thanksgiving Day might help. Is it possible that in some cases the cornucopia motif, the symbol of the earth's bounty, was included in an Album Quilt as a vote for a national Thanksgiving? I have no evidence for this except the knowledge that many Baltimorean ladies must have read *Godey's* and might perhaps have sympathized with Mrs. Hale's convictions.

Industriously investing hour upon hour in creating masterpiece quilts, the Baltimore quiltmakers must also have agreed with the *Godey* philosophy that creating beautiful home furnishings had an intrinsically high moral purpose.

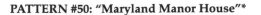

PATTERN #50: "Maryland Manor House"*

Type: Classic "Baltimore"

To make this block, refer to *Volume I*, Lessons 5 or 10.

Detail: *Volume I*, quilt #2.

Residential houses appear infrequently, but repeatedly in the classic Baltimore Album Quilts. The only one that I know to be labeled is captioned "The Bricklayer's Home," so we are set to wondering what the elegant place in our patterned block may be. In pursuing this question, I sought archival pictures of numerous buildings including the home of Thomas Wildey, founder of the Odd Fellows, and the Seven Stars Tavern where the Odd Fellows first met. Two factors quickly struck me in this search: that many public buildings of the early to mid-nineteenth century could be taken today as private residences, bearing as they do more resemblance to a

PATTERN #50: "Maryland Manor House"*

Second Page

house than to a great establishment. The second is that care has been taken to depict certain specific architectural details with clarity. Realism has been captured through the use of shaded fabric: the shadows of the gabled roofs, the perspective of the rolling lawn. On the other hand, the block's maker has allowed herself gross artistic license as witnessed by the bird, roughly one story high, and the towering flowers. This design conceit is common to American samplers as well and this house may be firmly grounded in the American schoolgirl sampler tradition.

That artistic license has been used seems important though, because this house looks rather like the house known as the Carroll Mansion, where Charles Carroll of Carrollton often stayed in Baltimore, on Front and Lombard Streets. Charles Carroll would have been an important personage to include in this vintage Baltimore Album Quilt. As Baltimore's most prosperous, most

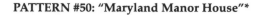

PATTERN #50: "Maryland Manor House"*

Third Page

prominent citizen, he was also one of Maryland's two first senators, the last living signer of the Declaration of Independence until his death in 1832, and performer of multiple important Masonic cornerstone laying ceremonies, including that of Baltimore's still standing Shot Tower and of the B. & O. Railroad. His death really marked the end of an era. For, as Alexis de Tocqueville remarked when visiting Carroll in 1831, "This race of men is disappearing after providing America with her greatest men. With them is lost the tradition of cultivated manners. The people become educated, knowledge extends, a middling ability becomes common. Outstanding talents and great characters are rare. Society is less brilliant and more prosperous." One senses that certain ladies of Baltimore felt the same, and hastened to memorialize their heroes in these quilts.

PATTERN #50: "Maryland Manor House"*

Fourth Page

In the chapter on picture blocks in *Volume II,* instructions are given on how to depict your own home or other significant buildings in your Album Quilt. This stately Maryland house would be a lovely edifice to begin for inclusion in your quilt in combination with picture blocks of your own design.

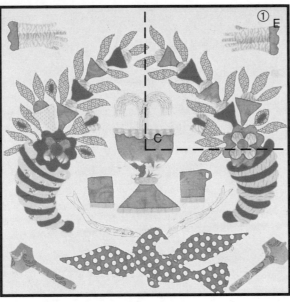

PATTERN #51: "Symbolic Fountain"*

Type: Classic "Baltimore"

To make this block, refer to *Volume I*, Lessons 5, 7, or 10.

Detail: *Volume I*, quilt #2.

I have seen fountains with two appellations in the classic Baltimore Album Quilts—the fountain of health, and the fountain of youth. Usually a bannered inscription names the distinction. Why did fountains become a motif in these quilts? The Christian symbolism of a fountain of water is associated with the Virgin Mary, "The Fountain of Living Waters." "For with thee is the Fountain of Life." Fountains were popular Renaissance motifs which brought back classical fountain depictions. But why might they have been popular in mid-nineteenth-century Baltimore? For one thing, fountains of water were a prime symbol of the temperance movement. The American Temperance

PATTERN #51: "Symbolic Fountain"*

Second Page

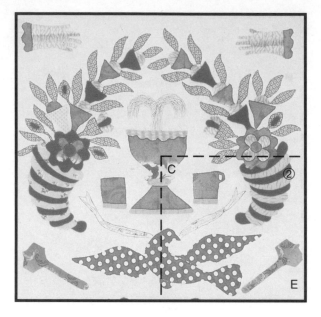

Union, started in 1826, held its first national convention in Philadelphia in 1833.

Increasingly, I read the symbolism of fraternal orders in these classic quilts. Fraternal orders printed charts that were basically teaching tools: each symbol being the "visible sign" of a moral or religious precept. Virtually the same fountain seen in this quilt block appears on the symbolic chart of the Knights Templars, a Masonic order. Temperance was an important element in the teachings of the Freemasons. Beneath the fountain are depicted two gavels which appear on Odd Fellow charts, and which to Masons symbolized the tool that would chip off the rough edges of vice and human foible, as one sought self-perfection. The clasped hands, too, were an Odd Fellows and a Freemason symbol, being a visible image or reminder of giving and receiving signs of recognition.

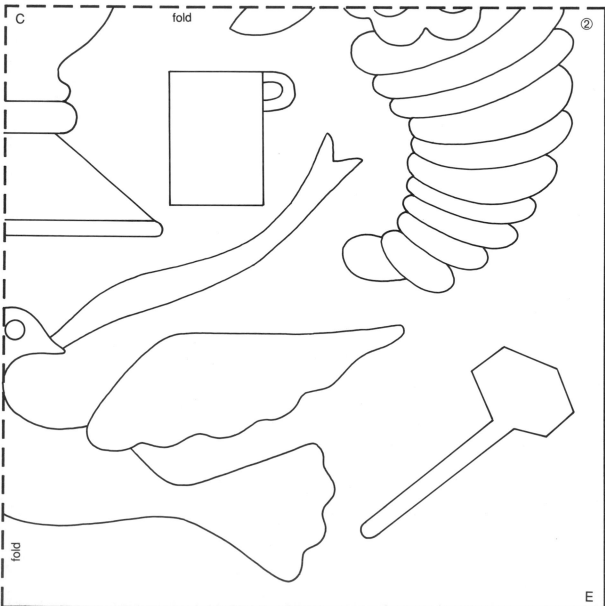

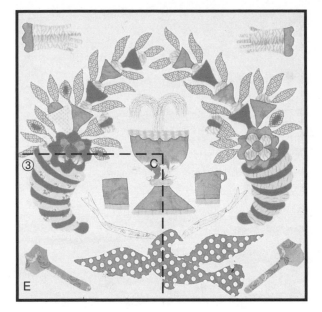

PATTERN #51: "Symbolic Fountain"*

Third Page

It is interesting to note that "The Fountain" is an antique quilting pattern as well. Ruth E. Finley shows an old template for this in *Old Patchwork Quilts and the Women Who Made Them* (plate 76). It is from a set of patterns "owned and used by my grandmother and her mother before her.... There was 'Fountain' wall-paper, 'Fountain' chintz, and 'Fountain' china. Doubtless there was also 'Fountain' quilting." Counting back three generations would place Mrs. Finley's heirloom quilting templates firmly into prime temperance movement times.

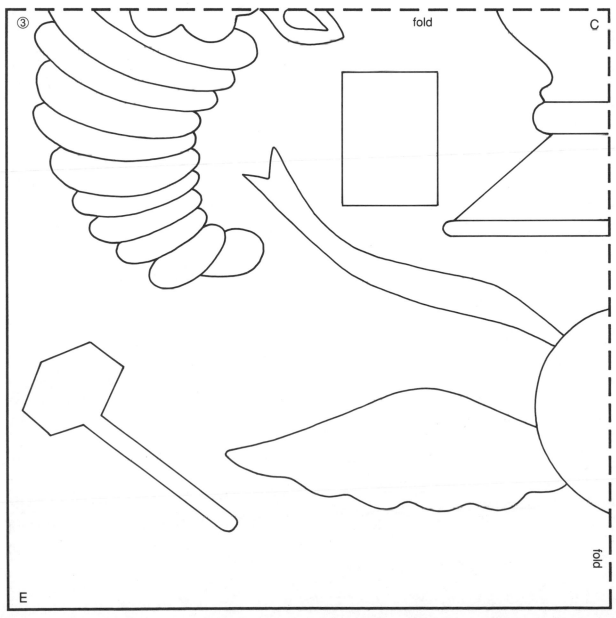

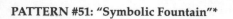

PATTERN #51: "Symbolic Fountain"*

Fourth Page

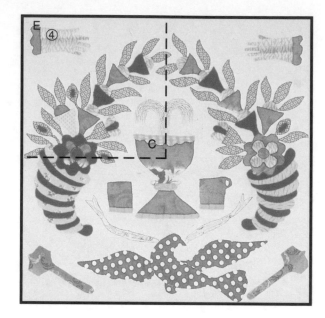

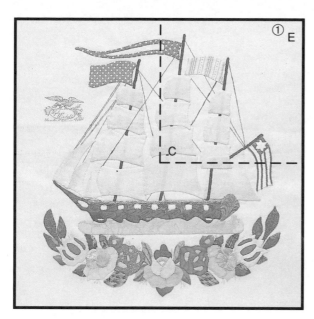

PATTERN #53: "Clipper Ship"*

Type: The ship is Classic Baltimore, captured exquisitely by Sylvia Pickell.

To make this block, refer to *Volume I*, Lessons 5, 9, or 10.

A magnificent clipper ship, the *Ann McKim*, like the one in this block, was built in Baltimore and launched in 1833. That event ushered in the era of the great clipper ships. By 1840, clippers, a rather ill-defined term (possibly derived from the expression "going at a fast clip") were skyrocketing in popularity on both sides of the Atlantic. Already, smaller ships of the genre were known as "Baltimore Clippers," and such impetus was given to the class by the California gold rush that 160 clippers were launched in four years to carry some 90,000 people west. American families—Bell, Hall, Steers, Webb, Collier, McKay, and Magoun—built clipper ships, and the Osgood, Marshall, Trask, Woodhouse, Delano, De Puyster, and Russell

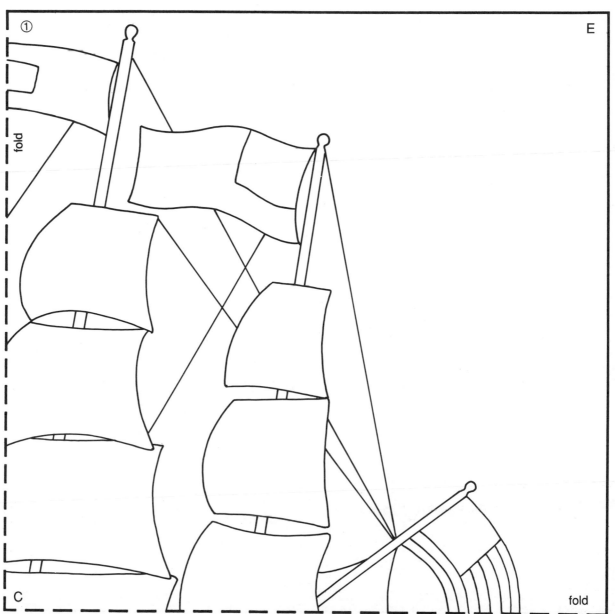

PATTERN #53: "Clipper Ship"*

Second Page

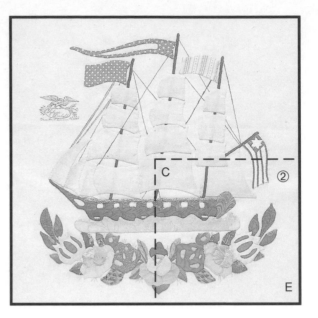

families provided many captains for the ships. After 1845, freight rates dropped and American shipbuilders switched to a smaller, less expensive "modified clipper" which never equalled the speed (up to 18 knots) of the original "extreme clipper." Clippers plied the high seas predominately between the eastern United States' ports and China. Beyond the gold rushes, and the opium and slave trades, the Chinese tea trade offered a potent motive for speed on the water. Because the fresh tea's flavor was perishable in a ship's hold, merchants offered annual prizes for the fastest delivery of the season's crop. *The Cutty Sark* (built in 1869) holds the record, 363 miles covered in one day in the annual tea-run race.

With her hull characteristically painted in bands of black and white, with dummy portholes painted in black, with great numbers of billowing sails and a long, sharp bow, the clipper ship was stunningly picturesque.

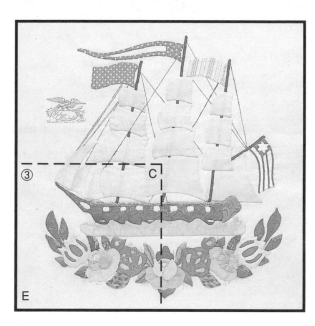

PATTERN #53: "Clipper Ship"*

Third Page

And what of the American flag she flew? In this block's original, the stars on the flag are shown by a five-petaled printed flower. More often they are depicted in the pattern of one great five-pointed star. This flag, the "Great Star Flag," was called by Oliver Wendell Holmes the "starry flower of liberty" and its petaled star shape (which was to become the flag of the American Merchant Marine) held sway from 1818 to the end of the Civil War. Though legislated guidelines for the precise design of the American flag were not set down until two decades into the twentieth century, the Great Star Flag in its manifold varieties was longer our flag than any since. It appeared in 1782 on the Great Seal of the United States and to this day the design appears above our national symbol on the dollar bill.

This magnificent Clipper Ship block is one of a small handful of gorgeous oceangoing vessels in the Baltimore

PATTERN #53: "Clipper Ship"*

Fourth Page

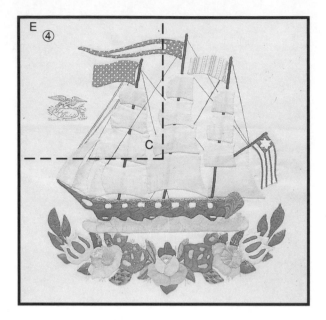

Album Quilts. Their manufacture reflected the mid-nineteenth-century shipbuilding revolution, then well underway in America. The dynamic changes (in construction, from wood to steel, and in propulsion, from sails to steam) in the mid-nineteenth century saw America dominate world commerce and the City of Baltimore prospered thereby.

Briton Samual Cunard founded the transatlantic Cunard Steamship line in 1840. Charles Dickens crossed the Atlantic to America on the *Britannia* in 1842, a two-cylinder side-lever paddle engine. On October 10, 1845, Secretary of the Navy George Bancroft oversaw the opening of the Annapolis Naval Academy at Fort Severn, not far from Baltimore. And the U.S. brought out its first transatlantic steamers in 1847 to run between New York and Bremen. Pride in all this progress is reflected in the Baltimore Album Quilts.

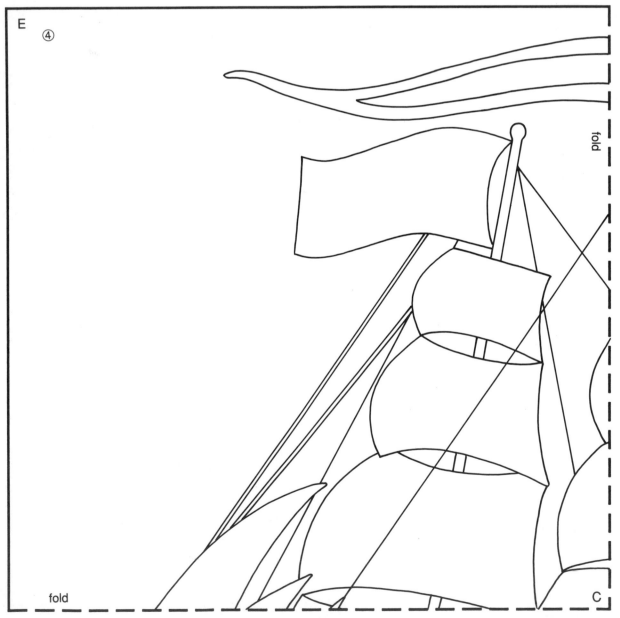

PATTERN #54: "Peacock Pastorale"*

Type: Classic "Baltimore"

To make this block, refer to *Volume I*, Lessons 1 or 2, 5 or 10.

Detail: *Volume I*, quilt #2.

The peacock in a lush bush is a recurring motif in the classic Baltimore Album Quilts. In my experience, it is mainly done in the ornate, more realistic, Victorian style, rather than in the sort of simplified version of block C-5 of quilt #3. You can see other versions of this same block in the Metropolitan's Baltimore Album Quilt (photo #26 in *Volume I*); in the quilt inscribed "To John and Rebecca Chamberlain" (shown in *Volume II*); and in quilt #2 in the Color Section. The slight variations among these three are part of the evidence which could mean different makers working in virtually the same style.

PATTERN #54: "Peacock Pastorale"*

Second Page

What is intriguing to me is that all three blocks could be reflecting the same design source. But the drafting of their shapes, fabric choices, and the layout of the motifs within the block all differ. And why peacocks? To begin with, no other bird calls for quite such an exotic display of fabric feathers. Beyond this, peacocks symbolize Immortality, and the "eyes" on its feathers represent the All-Seeing Eye of God. The peacock here is perched near an egg-filled nest, a sure omen of Fruitfulness and, in some cultures, Good Luck.

PATTERN #54: "Peacock Pastorale"*

Third Page

PATTERN #54: "Peacock Pastorale"*

Fourth Page

PATTERN #55: "Wreath and Dove II"*

Type: Classic "Baltimore"

To make this block, refer to *Volume I*, Lessons 5, 7, or 10.

In *Spoken Without a Word*, I speculated about what sort of bird this gracefully crested creature might be. Increasingly, I believe this is a stylization of a dove, not with a crest but with a little "fillip" to its head feathers. The body, the characteristic pose as God's messenger to Noah with the wild olive sprig in its beak, and its prevalence in these quilts would all seem to confirm this. The dove was a favorite symbol of the Daughters of Rebekah, the women Odd Fellows.

    The Odd Fellows Monitor and Guide says of the Dove, "This emblem presents to us important lessons for practice in life.... The cooing dove is the embodiment of

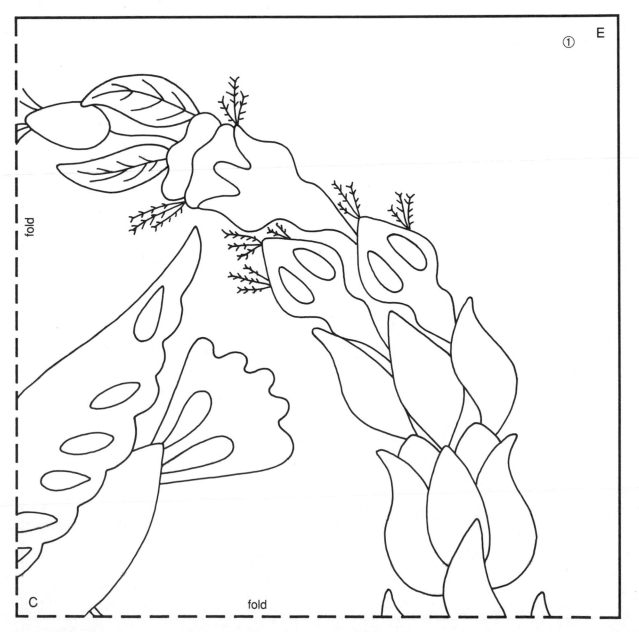

PATTERN #55: "Wreath and Dove II"*

Second Page

innocence and seems to injure nothing.... This emblem may also remind us of the Holy Spirit that descended, and in the form of a dove sat upon the head of the Savior as he stood upon the bank of the far-famed Jordan after he had been baptized by John.... This emblem tells us that we too may have the visits of that comforting messenger typified by Noah's dove. Yes, we may learn in its blessed influences on our hearts that the waters of Jehovah's wrath are assuaged, and that in the salvation provided, so beautifully typified by the ark, the offender may be reconciled with the offended."

PATTERN #55: "Wreath and Dove II"*

Third Page

Taken simply at face value, this is a beautiful block which any of us would be thrilled to put in our Album.

PATTERN #55: "Wreath and Dove II"*

Fourth Page

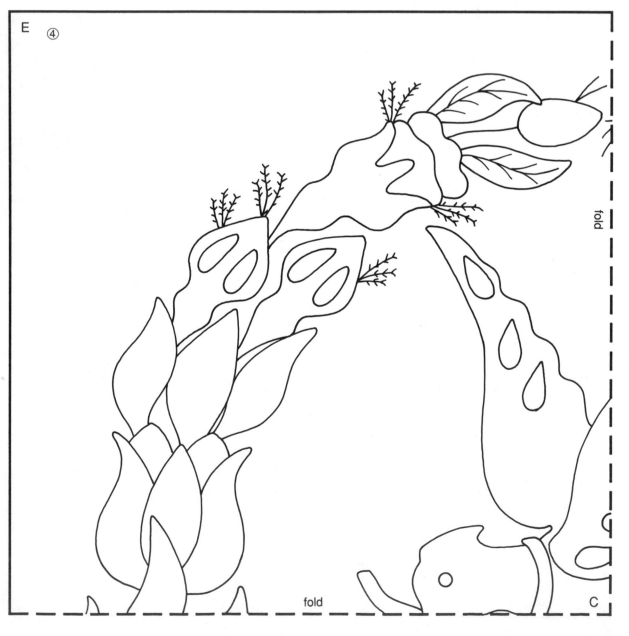

PATTERN #2: "Square Wreath with Fleur-de-Lis and Rosebuds"*

Type: Classic Baltimore from the Album "made by Mrs. Mary Everist, circa 1847-1850" in the collection of the Baltimore Museum of Art
To make this block, refer to *Volume I*, Lesson 1 or 4.

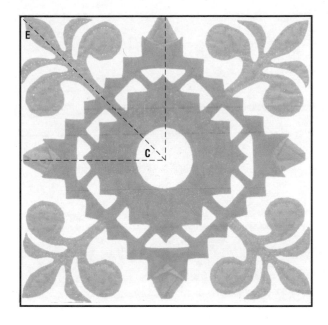

A seemingly unique version of the relentlessly popular "fleur-de-lis, rosebud, and square wreath" block, this one is both dramatic and intriguing. For, were one to read the fleur-de-lis as the national emblem of France, and the rose for Love, one might see this block as a tribute to the Marquis de Lafayette, "the hero of two continents," "the apostle of liberty." How? Lafayette's farewell tour of America in 1824-1825 produced a major artistic outpouring from Americans, Baltimoreans not the least. Lafayette was an ardent Mason, and his wife is said to have made the Masonic apron which George Washington wore to lay the cornerstone of the Nation's Capitol. Bespeaking Masonry, the center of this block reads almost as a "geometry sampler" with the square, the circle, and triangles. And geometry is "the basis on which the superstructure of freemasonry is erected," according to *The True Masonic Chart*.

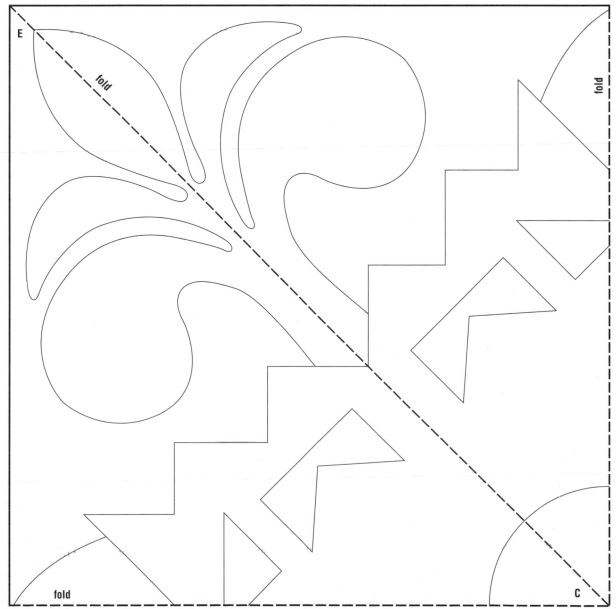

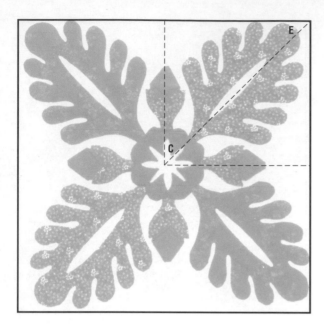

PATTERN #3: "Crossed Pine Cones and Rosebuds"*

Type: Classic Baltimore
To make this block, refer to *Volume I*, Lesson 5.

There are innumerable versions of pine cone blocks. The fact that this object was so oft repeated in the classic Baltimore Album Quilts, yet was sometimes almost homely in rendition was, for me, an early clue to its symbolic intent. Pine cones symbolize Fertility or Fruitfulness because of the pine's many seeds. The pine tree was an important symbol for freedom in Revolutionary times, and the wooden pole often seen in patriotic eagle blocks would be the pine "liberty pole." Using the terms "pine" and "cone" differently, Dr. Dunton in *Old Quilts* (p. 209) writes of their ancient symbolism (Fertility and the Creator) in connection with the date palm.

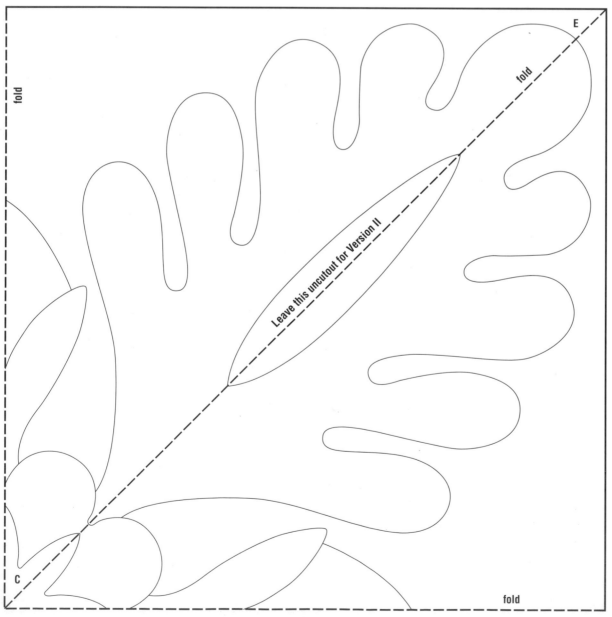

Leave this uncutout for Version II

PATTERN #4: "Joy Nichol's Rose of Sharon"*

Type: "Beyond" Baltimore
To make this block, refer to *Volume I*, Lesson 9 and 10.

This pattern, which I call the Rose of Sharon but which, according to Cuesta Benberry, may be the President's Wreath, recurs repeatedly in the classic Baltimore Album Quilts. By either name, its inclusion would be significant as well as beautiful. Joy's fabric use in this version of her design is rich, textural in appearance, and charming.

PATTERN #6: "Acorn and Oak Leaf Frame"*

Type: "Beyond" Baltimore
To make this block, refer to *Volume I*, Lesson 1, 2, or 11.

Botanical themes provide an endless source for designing your own picture-block frames. Because the acorn symbolizes Longevity and Immortality, the oak's leaves, Courage, and the oak tree, Strength against Adversity, this seemed the perfect choice of magic with which to wrap this portrait of my husband and me. Any one of the picture-block frames would also make an ideal enclosure for an inscription.

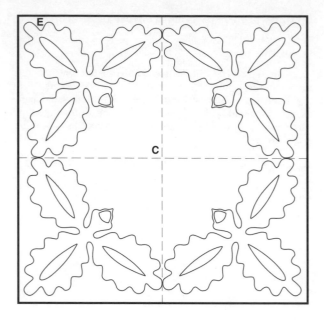

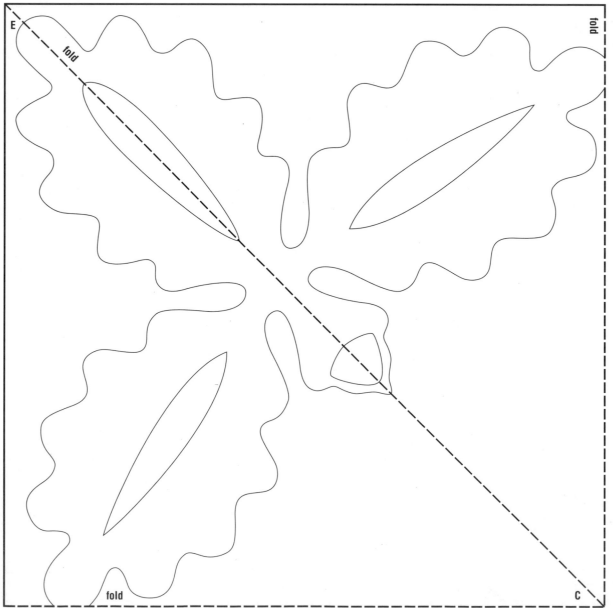

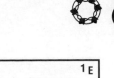

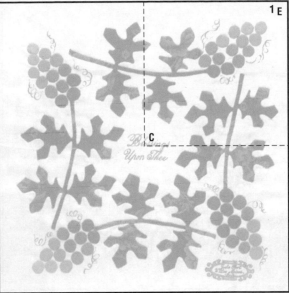

PATTERN #10: "Squared Grapevine Wreath"*

Type: Classic Baltimore from the quilt in the collection of the Baltimore Museum of Art
To make this block, refer to *Volume I*, Lessons 1, 2, and 9.

This block fascinated me. It was such an unusual (infrequent, but repeated) stylization by which to depict grapes. I speculated that it would have made a good teaching block with stems, circles, points—and wondered if the pattern had been taught as an appliqué sample at some ladies' academy of the period, one accessible to Baltimoreans. It seemed almost like mental telepathy, then, when a version of this block caught my eye in a quilt labeled "Oxford Female Seminary Album Quilt." To complete this pattern, rotate the grape bunch clockwise.

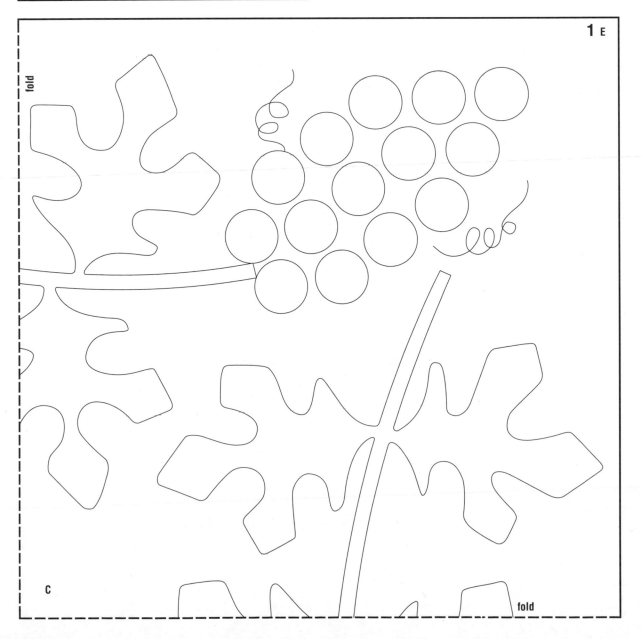

PATTERN #10: "Squared Grapevine Wreath"*

(Second Page)

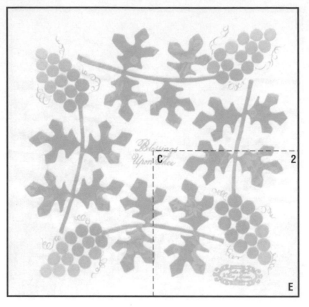

Blessings Upon Thee

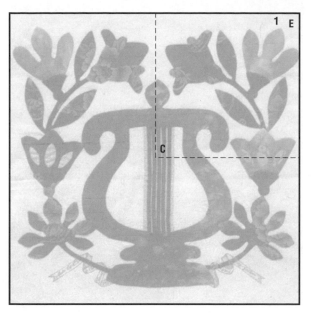

PATTERN #11: "Numsen Family Lyre"*

Type: Classic Baltimore
To make this block, refer to *Volume I*, Lessons 5 and 10. See also *Baltimore Album Quilts — Historic Notes and Antique Patterns*, Appendix I.

I first saw this simple and very sculptural lyre in a floral wreath in the Numsen I quilt, then again in the Numsen II quilt in the same fabrics (see *Volume III*), and again in these fabrics in yet a third quilt recently discovered in the Virginia quilt search but with no name written upon it. In the Numsen II quilt, this block bears the inscription, "Sophia C. Numsen." Based on a Numsen family geneaology, at least four quilts bear Numsen family names. According to that geneaology, young Sophia—and some friends who married into the family—were of a marrying age when those quilts were made. Perhaps this graphic and relatively quick block was the one Sophia repeated to give the others for their

PATTERN #11: "Numsen Family Lyre"*

(Second Page)

Albums? I have thought that if I needed such a quick and easy block for giving, the Ruched Rose Lyre block from *Volume I* would be my favorite. By using cutwork appliqué for all the green, and red soutache for the lyre strings, this Numsen Family Lyre was equally appealing to make.

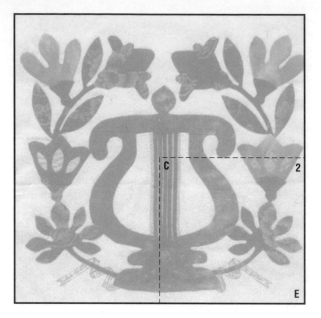

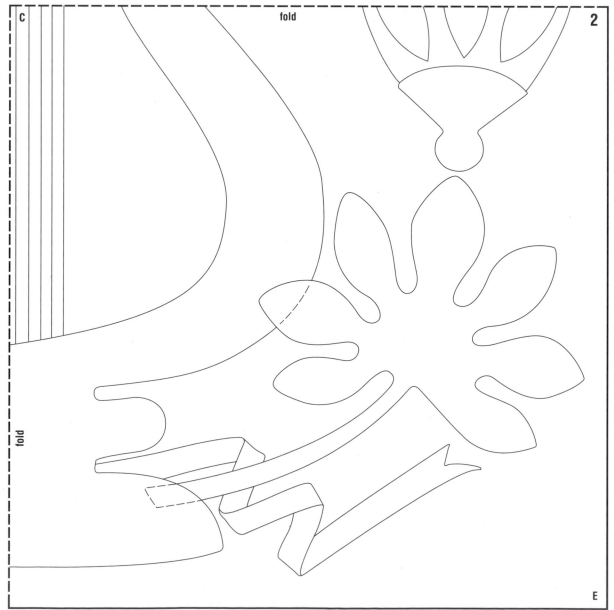

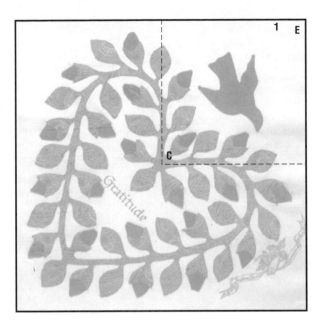

PATTERN #14: "Rosebud Wreathed Heart"*

Type: "Beyond" Baltimore
To make this block, refer to *Volume I*, Lessons 1 or 2, 5 and 6.

This pattern is based on an upright rosebud-wreathed heart, block C-1 in the Baltimore Album Quilt, 1847-1848, made for Reverend Dr. George C. M. Roberts, and now in the collection of Lovely Lane Museum, Baltimore (see Photo 4-15). I designed this version as a diagonal block that would guide the eye inward from the outside corners of a quilt. Two models for this block were made by Ellie Dawson and Jo Anne Parisi in the "Odense Album."

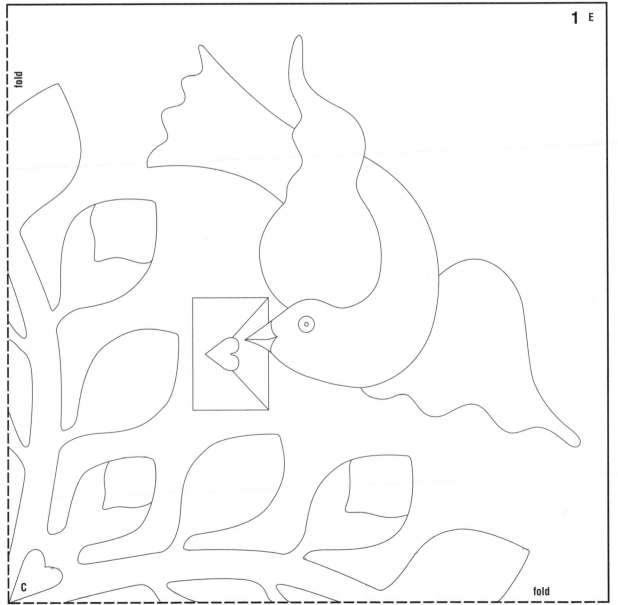

PATTERN #14: "Rosebud Wreathed Heart"*

(Second page)

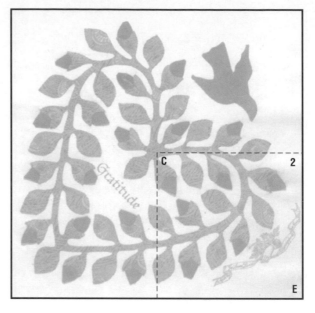

PATTERN #14: "Rosebud Wreathed Heart"*

(Third page)

PATTERN #14: "Rosebud Wreathed Heart"*

(Fourth page)

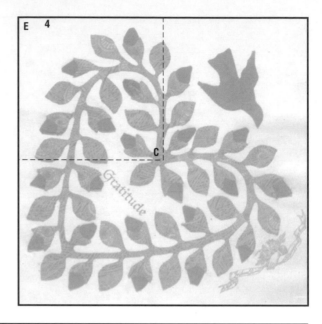

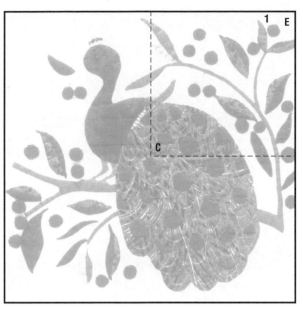

PATTERN #18: "Joy Nichol's Peacock"*

Type: "Beyond" Baltimore
To make this block, refer to *Volume I*, Lesson 10.

The exotic, magnificently decorative peacock was a favorite tropical bird for inclusion in one's Album Quilt. Joy Nichols designed this elegant pattern. She presents it splendidly here out of an evocative print with the tail feathers stem-stitch outlined in gold thread and their "eyes" fashioned of applied purple circles. The bird's eye is a bright black button bead which echoes the dimensionality of the stuffed cherries.

There is a possibility that peacocks were so common in the classic Album Quilts for symbolic reasons as well as aesthetic ones. Legend held that the peacock's body does not decay, making of them a visible sign of the concept of immortality. And this, of course is what symbols do — provide a visible sign of something that is invisible. In Christian iconography, too, the hundred tail-feather eyes symbolize the All-Seeing Eye of the Church and of God. The All-Seeing Eye of God was an important precept of

PATTERN #18: "Joy Nichol's Peacock"*

(Second page)

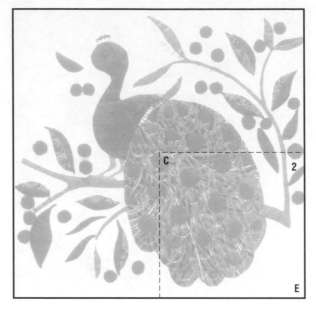

the Freemasons and the Odd Fellows whose symbolism so permeates many of these quilts. And thus one cannot dismiss the possibility that where the All-Seeing Eye of God is represented, it might have fraternal order connotations. Stuff of the spirit seems to have been so important to the Victorian quiltmakers: friendship, truth, remembrance, devotion, loyalty, charity, divine music, immortality, religion, patriotism, glory, duty, honor, country, courage, faith, hope, love, benevolence, sweet character, good deeds…. Perhaps these symbols and the stuff of the spirit they represent connect us to these quilts more powerfully than we care to admit or can even understand.

PATTERN #18: "Joy Nichol's Peacock"*

(Third page)

PATTERN #18: "Joy Nichol's Peacock"*

(Fourth page)

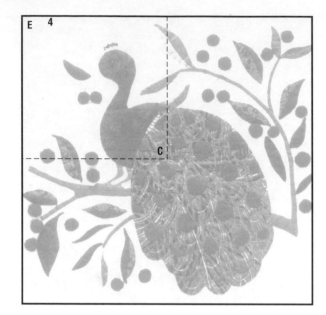

PATTERN #19: "Updegraf Basket, Book, and Bird"*

Type: Classic Baltimore
To make this block, refer to *Volume I*, Lesson 10.

Baskets, books, birds — classic themes in classic quilts. Seemingly most often labeled Bible or Holy Bible, some books are simply labeled, as is this one, "Album." And so we come back to the Album. But now one's sense of the Album and its importance to the Victorians has caught our attention, connected us to them. And that, it seems, is what Album Quilts did and do — affirm, remember, "connect." At their best, Album Quilts were artfully presented collections that pushed the limits of variations on a theme. This block's designer must have been particularly pleased to extend the variety of Album presentations to this one where the book is presented gifted in a bouquet, an album itself within an Album!

PATTERN #19: "Updegraf Basket, Book, and Bird"*

(Second page)

PATTERN #19: "Updegraf Basket, Book, and Bird"*

(Third page)

PATTERN #19: "Updegraf Basket, Book, and Bird"*

(Fourth page)

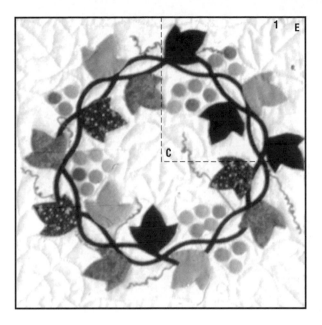

PATTERN #20: "Jeanne's Grapevine Wreath"*

Type: "Beyond" Baltimore
To make this block, refer to *Volume I*, Lessons 9 and 10.

Jeanne Benson designed this winning block for the 1984 contest based on *Spoken Without a Word*. While it is entirely of her own design, the Victorian quiltmakers would undoubtedly have loved it. For it has characteristics they seem so to have admired: a balanced asymmetry, an airiness to the pattern, a pleasing naturalism to the stylization, and what appears to have been their very favorite Album Quilt fruit, the grapevine. Jeanne's soft, subtle colors work well with the brighter ones in *Volume I*'s quilt #7, where this block appears.

PATTERN #20: "Jeanne's Grapevine Wreath"*

(Second page)

To complete this pattern's left half:
Flop pattern units 1 & 2, making unit 2 the top half and
unit 1 the bottom half.

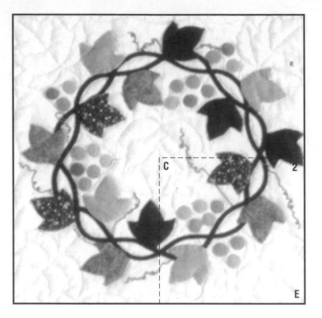

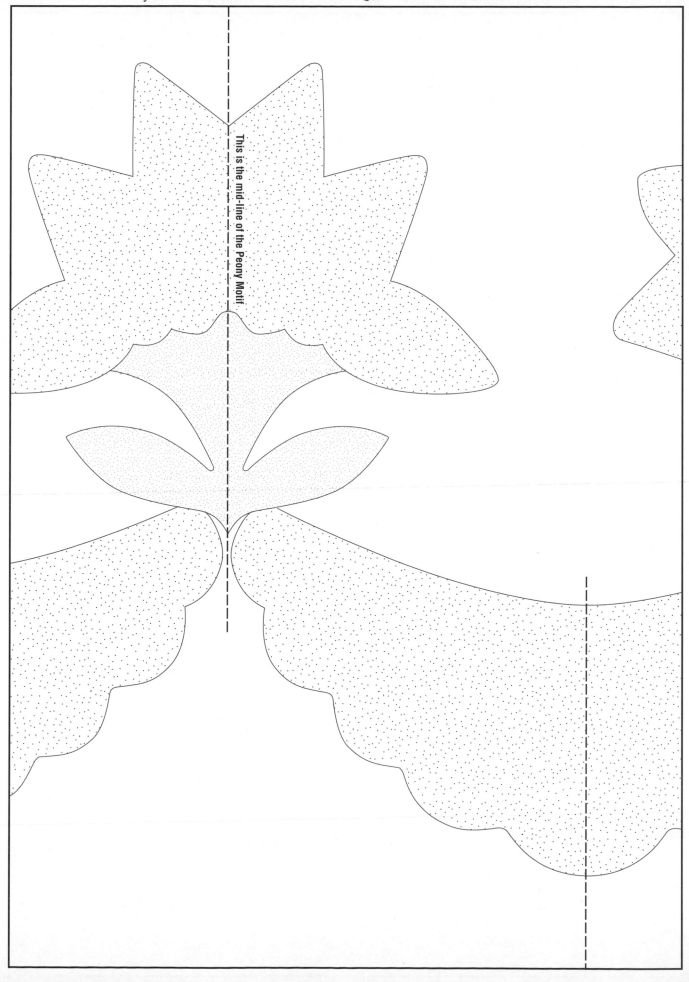

This is the mid-line of the Peony Motif.

PATTERN #22: Peony and Hammock Border (2)

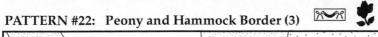

This line bisects the border's corner

PATTERN #23:   Hammock and Bow Border (1)

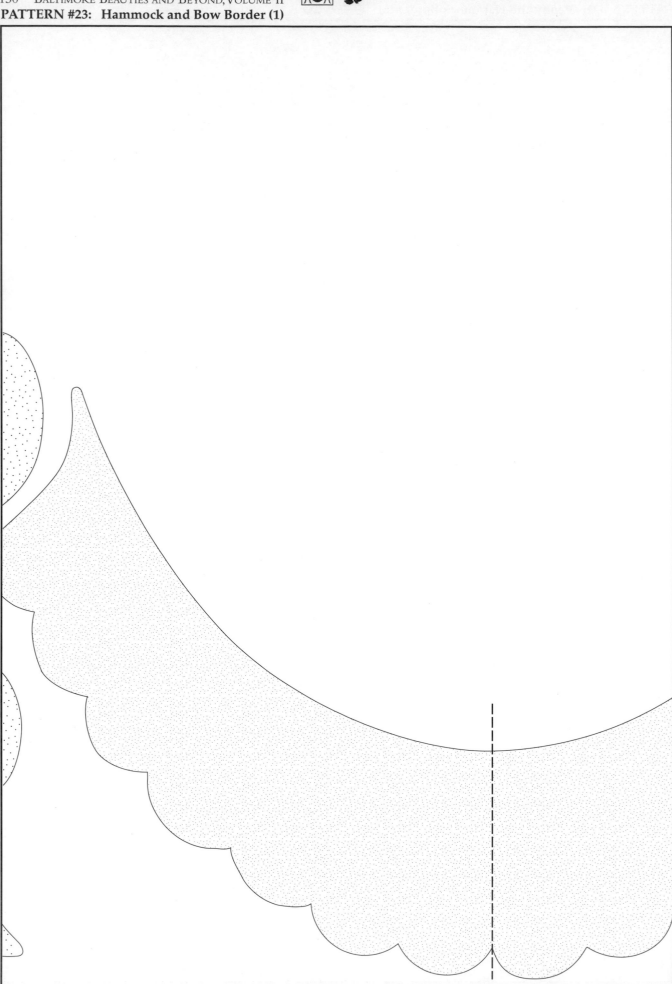

PATTERN #23: Hammock and Bow Border (3)

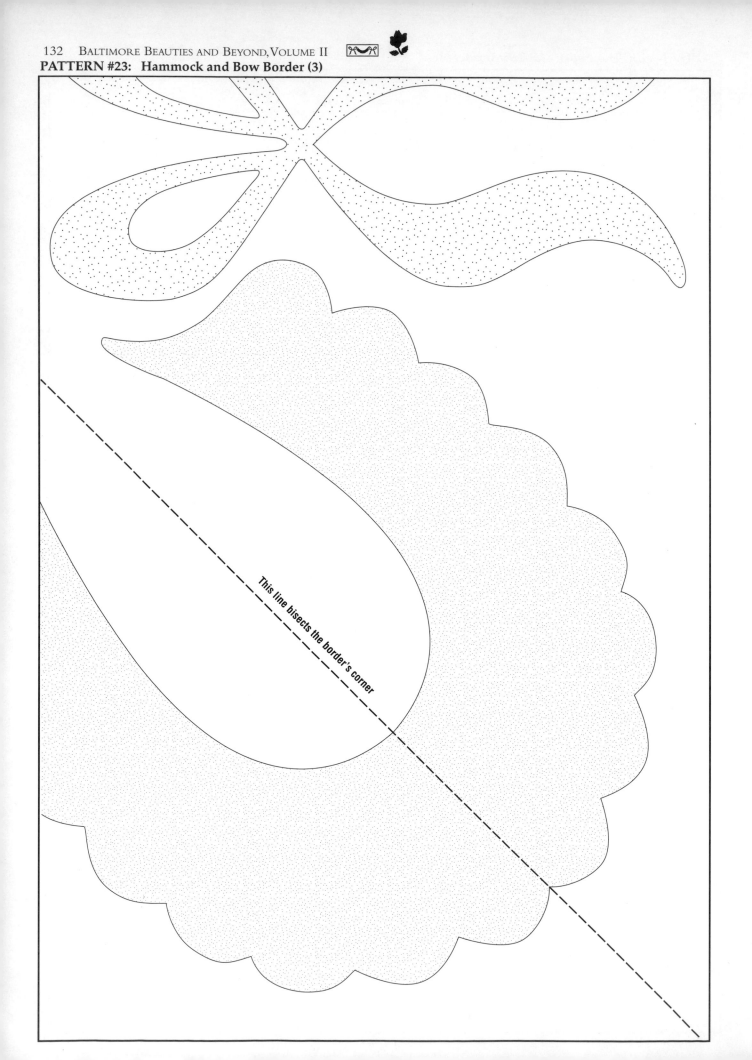

This line bisects the border's corner

PATTERN #24: Scalloped Border

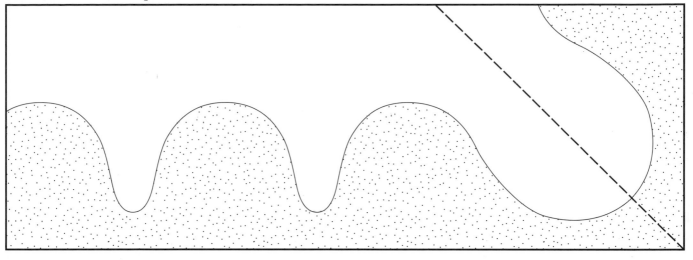

PATTERN #25: Stepped Border (four steps)

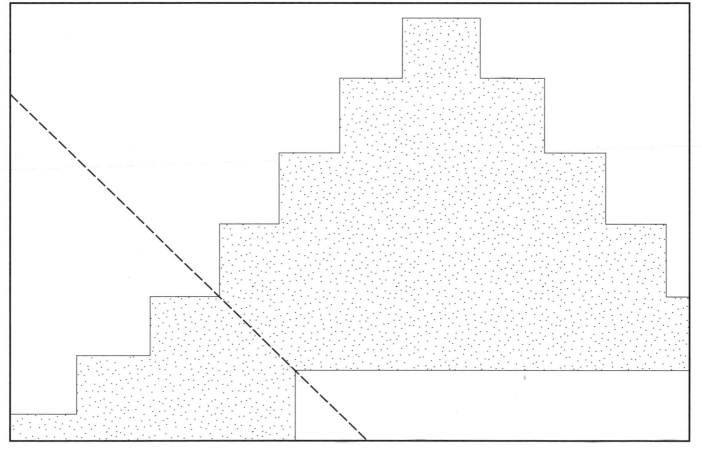

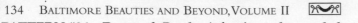

PATTERN #26:   Dogtooth Border (of a size to be used alone)

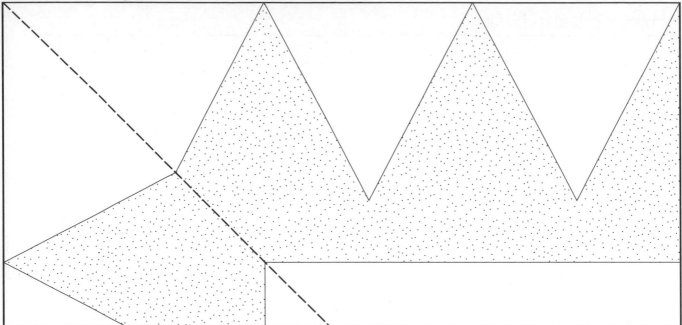

PATTERN #27:   Stepped Border (six steps)

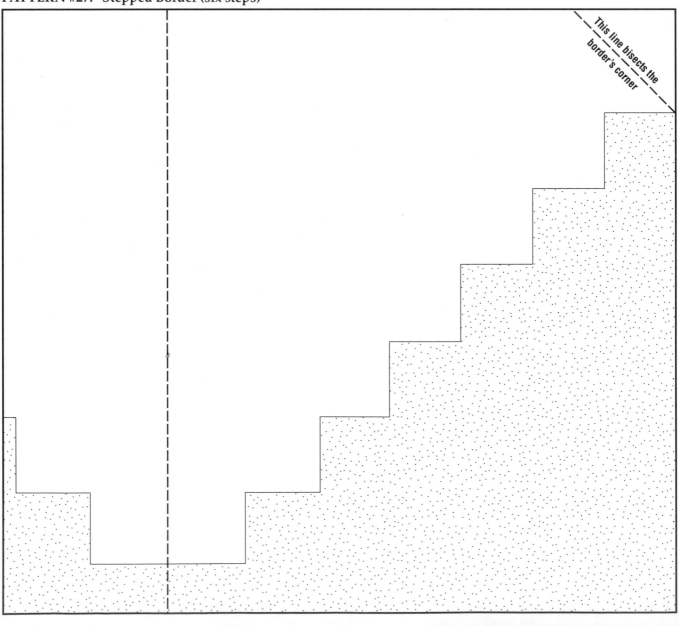

This line bisects the border's corner

PATTERN #28:   Ruffled Border

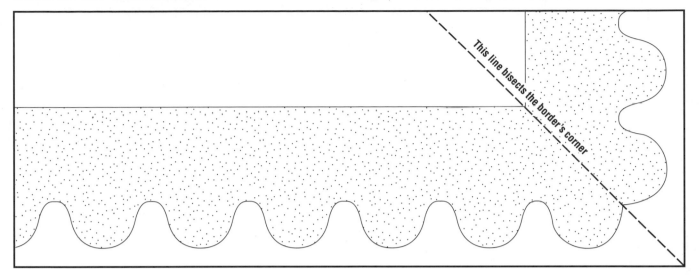

PATTERN #29:   Dogtooth Triangle Border I

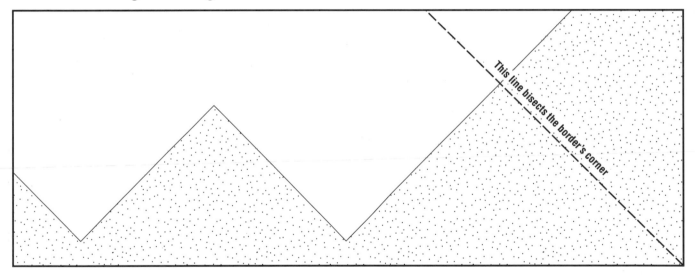

PATTERN #30:   Dogtooth Triangle Border II

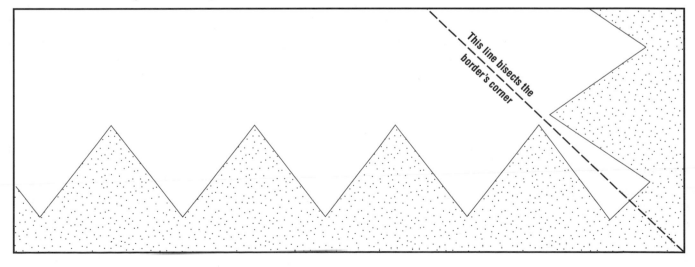

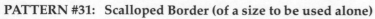

PATTERN #31: Scalloped Border (of a size to be used alone)

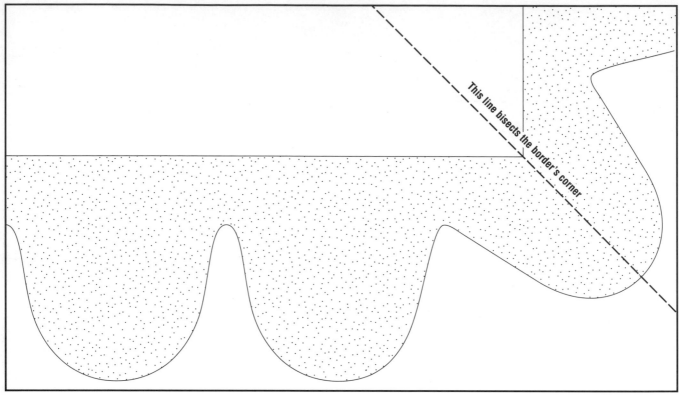

PATTERN #32: Stepped Border (three steps)

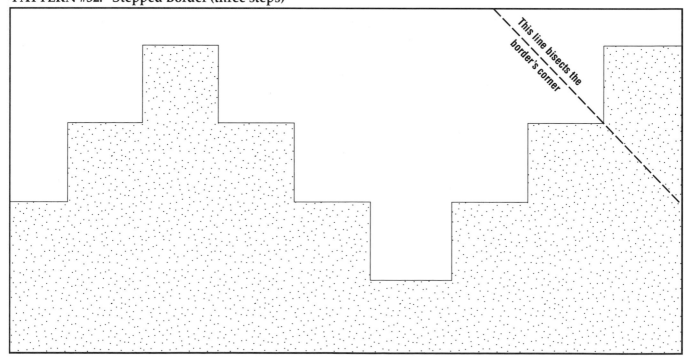

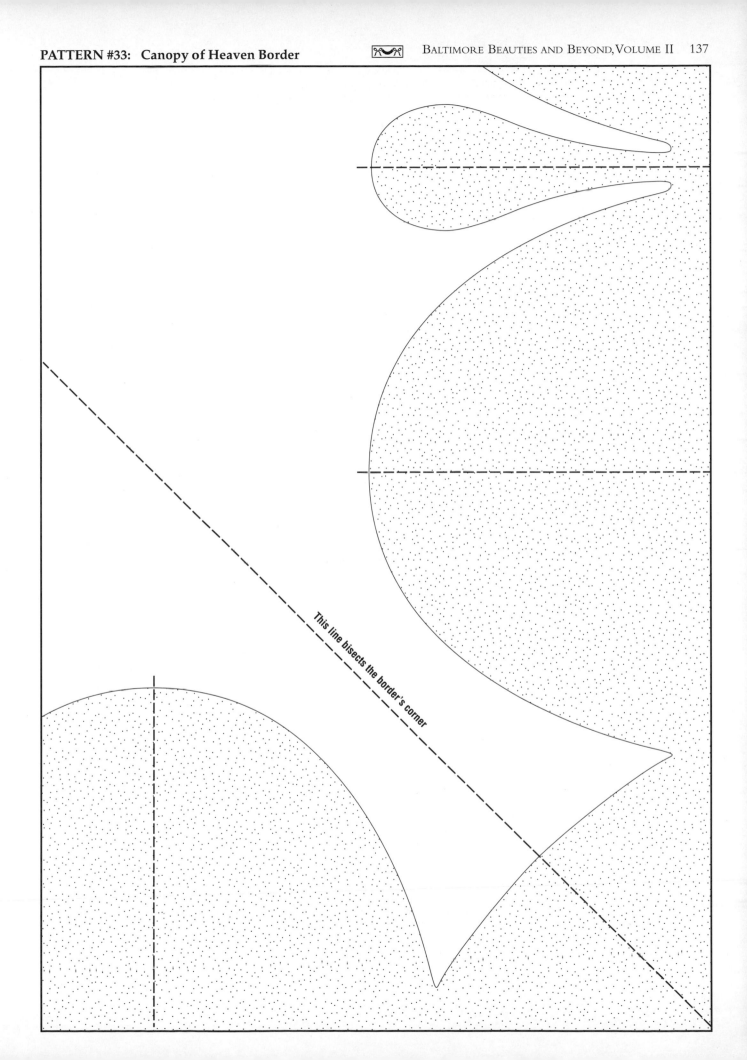

This line bisects the border's corner

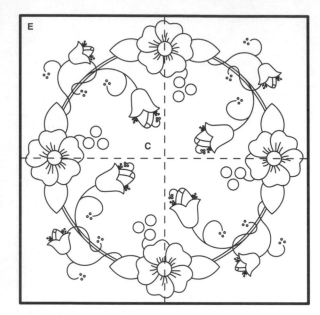

PATTERN #1: "Roses are Red"

Type: "Beyond"; Designed by Gwendolyn LeLacheur

To make this block, refer to Lessons 3, 7, and 8; in *Volume I,* Lessons 6 and 9.

    This wreath has a relaxed, inviting look. Gwen LeLacheur who designed the pattern has used fabrics that make this block sing. She began with the superfine stem, then the leaves and large-petaled flowers. The embroidery in chain stitch, blanket stitch and French knots is all done in two strands of ginger-colored floss.

Key:
1. Superfine stems 2. Blanket-stitched leaves
3. Petaled flower in graduated shades
4. Folded Circle Roses (Use Template A for inner buds, B for outer buds.) 5. Embroidered details: Stem stitch and French knots
6. Stitched rose moss 7. Stem-stitched petal detail

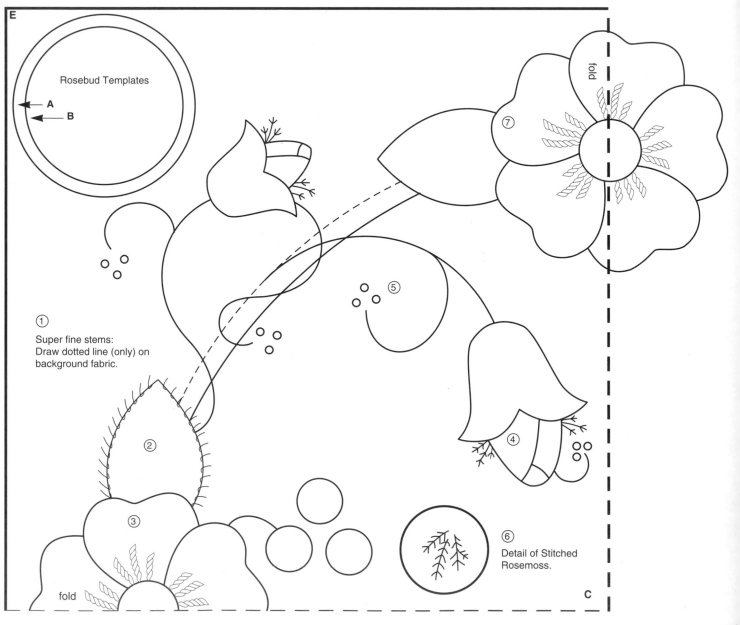

Rosebud Templates

A
B

① Super fine stems: Draw dotted line (only) on background fabric.

②

③

⑤

④

⑦

fold

⑥ Detail of Stitched Rosemoss.

fold

PATTERN #2: "I Promised You a Rose Garden"

Type: "Beyond"; Designed by Gwendolyn LeLacheur

To make this block, refer to Lesson 8; in *Volume I*, Lessons 9 and 10.

This lovely original's repetitious nature makes the design quickly graspable. But the texture of the multi-petaled roses and the swirl of the small (two strands floss) embroidered stems, keeps one fascinated. Mrs. Numsen's Rose I is featured in the eight large roses. Twelve folded rosebuds (1¾"-diameter circles in color #3) are supported by stem-stitched green stems and accented with red French knots. Begin by making a superfine stem from a ¾"-wide piece of bias. Make leaves with a freezer paper template on the inside. For the full-blown rose (Mrs. Numsen's Rose I), follow the directions in Lesson 8. Finish with the embroidery noted on the pattern.

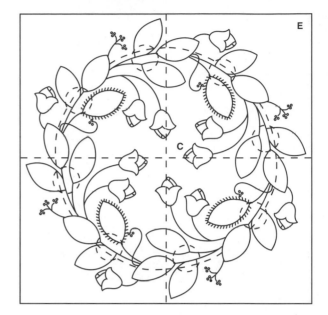

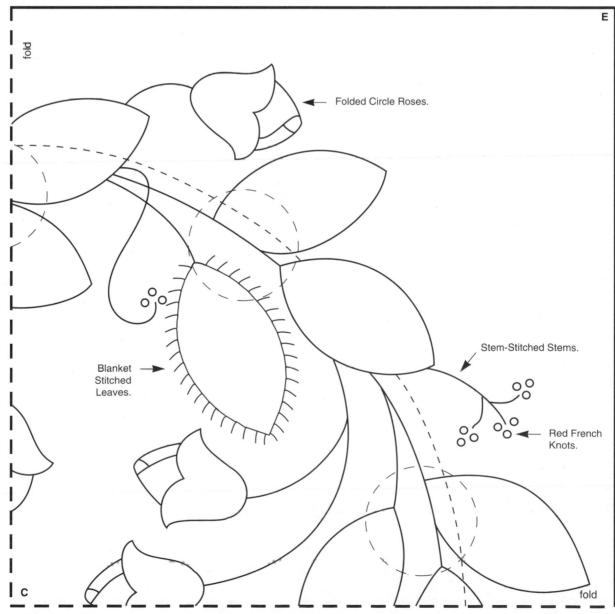

Folded Circle Roses.

Stem-Stitched Stems.

Blanket Stitched Leaves.

Red French Knots.

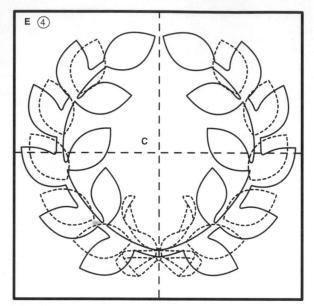

PATTERN #3: "Wreath of Folded Ribbon Roses"

Type: "Beyond"; Designed by the author

To make this block, refer to Lessons 5 and 7; in *Volume I,* Lessons 2 and 6.

This is a delightfully simple block, elegantly done in a carefully chosen green cloth. Choose a medium to large-scale print, which breaks the green up a bit and gives the impression of a bit more complexity than there actually is in the wreath's straightforward shape. P & B Textiles' *Baltimore Beauties* green "Ombré Leaves" is excellent for this block. The rosebuds, too, look more lifelike folded in shaded wire ribbon or mottled cloth.

PATTERN #3: "Wreath of Folded Ribbon Roses"

Second page

This strong, easy-to-construct block showcases a calligraphed inscription or an inked drawing at its center. *Baltimore Beauties and Beyond, Volume II* teaches you how to do this. Alternatively, elegant calligraphed sentiments border P & B's "Classic Album Cloth," and one of these, framed by a reverse appliquéd oval, would be this block's perfect finishing touch. *Baltimore Beauties Fabric Notes:* P & B Textiles invited my design consultation on a 38-piece fabric line named *Baltimore Beauties* in honor of this series. Our needs (both in replicating old Baltimore and in taking it beautifully beyond) helped determine that fabric's style. For this reason, *Baltimore Beauties Fabric Notes* are included, where possible, on subsequent patterns.

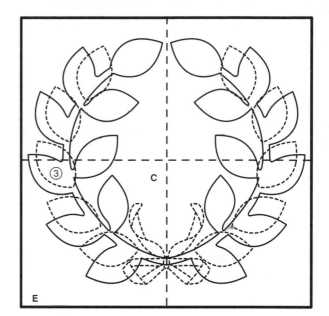

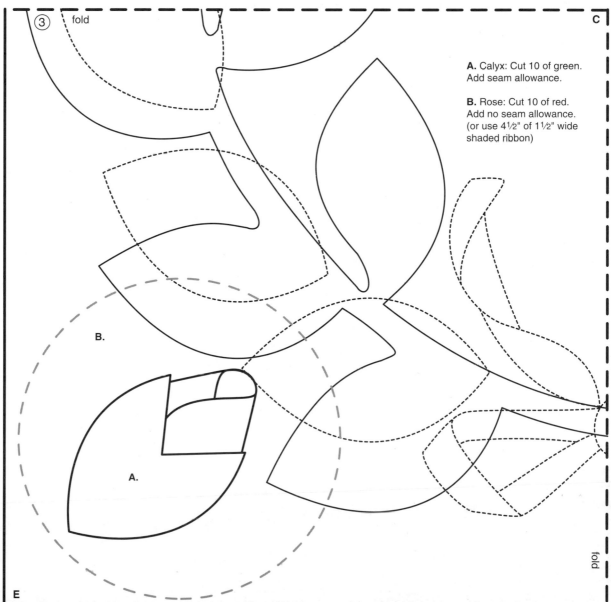

A. Calyx: Cut 10 of green. Add seam allowance.

B. Rose: Cut 10 of red. Add no seam allowance. (or use 4½" of 1½" wide shaded ribbon)

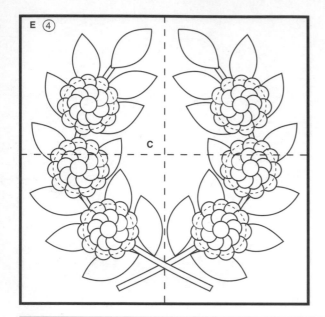

PATTERN #4: "Crown of Ten Penny Roses"

Type: "Beyond"; Designed by the author

To make this block, refer to Lessons 4 and 7; in *Volume I,* Lessons 9 and 10.

The ten-penny nomen derives from the dime-sized circle petals on these roses. This flower's basted-only antique original repeated twill-like Turkey red cotton petals. Debbie Ballard stitched this bloom in a plethora of red textures against a backdrop of dramatic green prints. The effect is dynamic! Office dots (³/₄" diameter) ease the stitching as Lesson 4 explains. For stem placement, draw only the dashed outer line of the stems on the background cloth. For flower placement, draw the six dotted circles.

Baltimore Beauties Fabric Notes: For the leaves, mix greens from these P & B designs: Ombré Leaves,

PATTERN #4: "Crown of Ten Penny Roses"

Second page

Ombré Ferns, Baltimore Rose, and Vermiculates. Two strips of the Ombré Leaves, cut on the bias, then seamed together to form chevrons, make ideal "split leaves." So does one strip of Ombré Leaves sewn (right or wrong side up) to a Vermiculate green.

For the Rose Petals, use the same patterns just listed, but in shades of Victoria Red or Baltimore Blue.

For the Background Cloth, use P & B's "Classic Album Cloth," which reproduces the words from Lesson 2 in *Baltimore Beauties and Beyond, Volume II.* Perhaps one of these is the perfect finishing touch for this block's center.

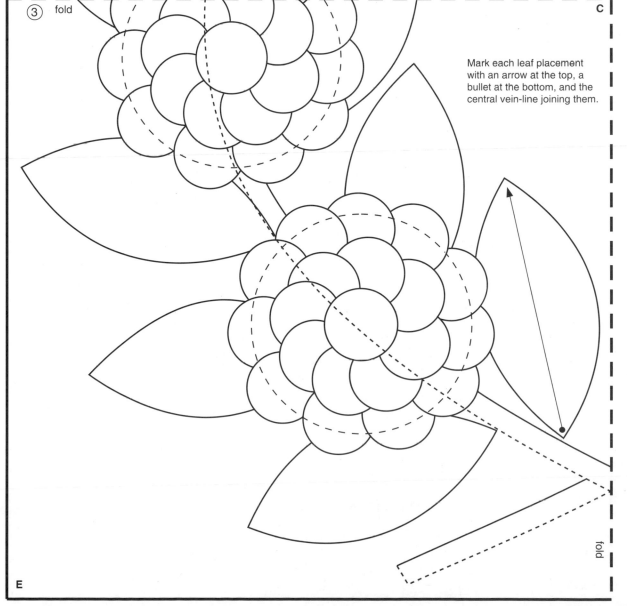

③ fold

Mark each leaf placement with an arrow at the top, a bullet at the bottom, and the central vein-line joining them.

C

fold

E

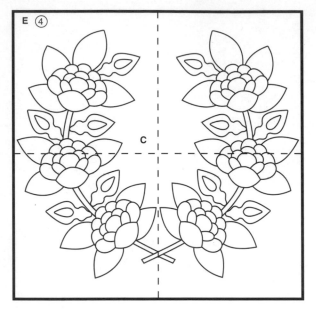

PATTERN #5: "Crown of Quilted Roses"

Type: "Beyond"; Designed by the author

To make this block, refer to Lesson 7; in *Volume I*, Lessons 9 and 10.

Here, rich red *crêpe de Chine* silk echoes the velvety depth of real roses. This style of stuffed-rose block was typically made in a simple two fabric red/green palette. Marjo Hodges quilted, then outlined each bud and each rose, petals and all, with the stem-stitch (or the outline stitch) done in silk buttonhole twist. If you backstitch-quilt the rose, you will be both quilting and embroidering it at the same time. Echoing the botanical authenticity seen in some antebellum Album blocks, Marjo embroidered the greenery with soft loden green floss twined with a beige thread. She's come delightfully close to the look of a real rose thorn streaked with red or beige.

Mark each leaf with a placement arrow and bullet.

A. Detail: Leaf Embroidery.

PATTERN #5: "Crown of Quilted Roses"

Second page

The original straight-stitching on buds and leaves would likely have been done in wool. One also sees closely worked patches of straight-stitched silk highlights on the plump round of the petals. The wool straight stitches may have been related to the concurrent Victorian fad of Berlin Work, a sort of needlepoint done in tapestry yarn. *Pattern transfer suggestion for any crown or wreath with vertically symmetrical leaves:* Make a complete (two-tipped) freezer paper leaf pattern, but snip the bottom end blunt for easy removal of the template. This allows you to mass produce the leaves all in one size and shape, but still place them at different depths guided by your placement arrows and bullets. On designs where you want to vary the leaf fabrics, it means that you can make up lots of leaves, then play with their arrangement on the block.

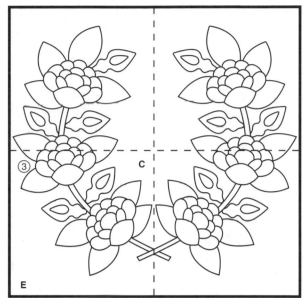

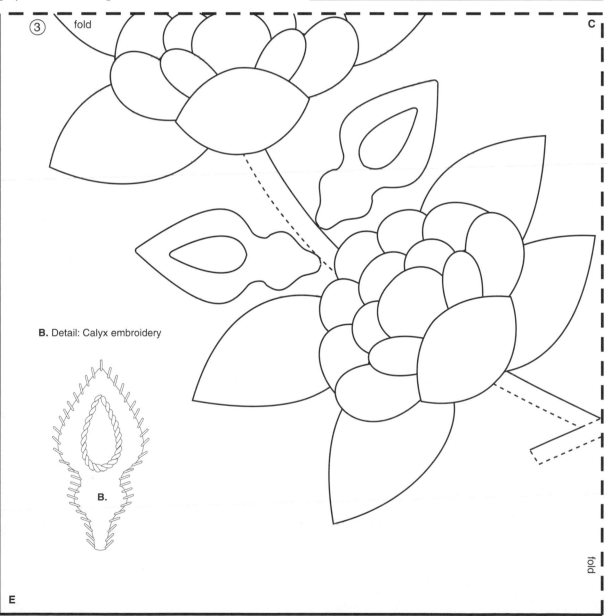

B. Detail: Calyx embroidery

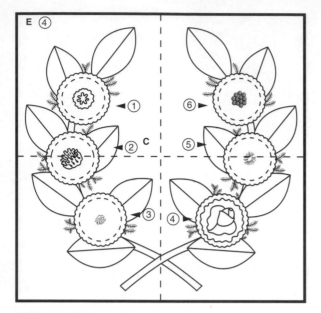

PATTERN #6: "Crown of Ruched Roses"

Type: "Beyond"; Designed by the author

To make this block, refer to Lesson 7; in *Volume I*, Lessons 9 and 10.

This pattern was inspired by the picture of a circa 1852 Album Quilt made for Miss Isabella Battee and now owned by the Baltimore Museum of Art. I've combined that block's crown of ruched roses with the yellow-centered ruched roses from another Album. Lesson 7 teaches all the delights of this pattern from two-toned, embroidered leaves, to changing colors within a rose and giving each rose a different center. This is a fancywork block to linger over and enjoy! The key on the facing page tells which center was used on each rose, reading the roses counterclockwise from the top left.

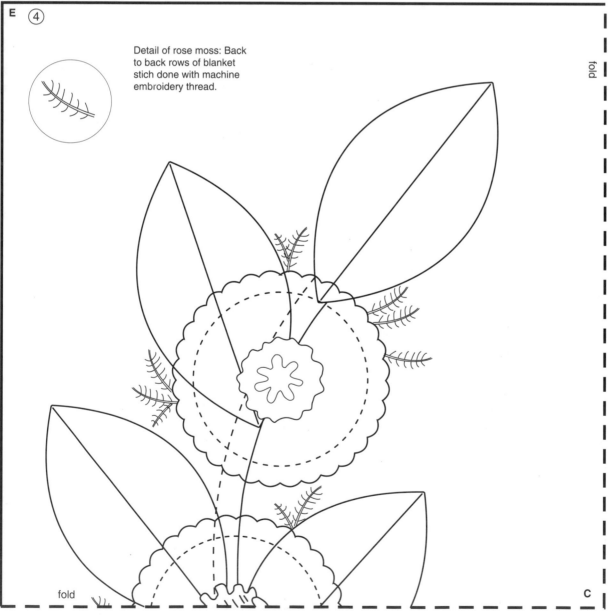

Detail of rose moss: Back to back rows of blanket stich done with machine embroidery thread.

E ④

fold

fold

C

PATTERN #6: "Crown of Ruched Roses"

Second page

Key to the Ruched Roses' Novelty Centers:

Blossom #1: Mrs. Numsen's Fringed Center (gold China Silk) tucked into a Yo-Yo Center (hand-dyed silk)

Blossom #2: Yo-Yo Center

Blossom #3: Turkeywork (wool yarn, looped, then shorn off flat)

Blossom #4: Ruched Rose base topped by a Rolled Rose made by Method #2 (see Lesson 1).

Blossom #5: Mrs. Numsen's Fringed Center (corn-silk colored cotton).

Blossom #6: French Knot Center

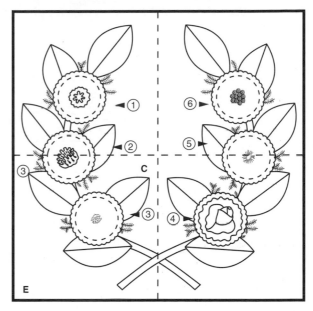

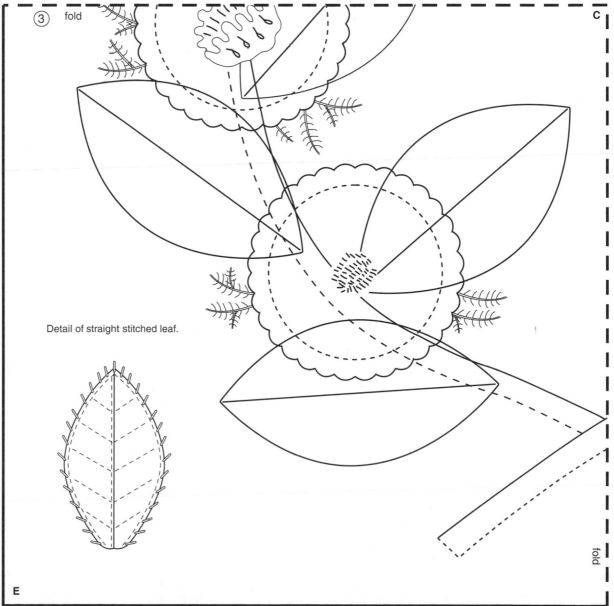

Detail of straight stitched leaf.

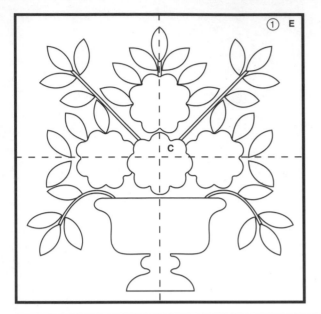

PATTERN #10: "Vase of Full-Blown Roses I"

Type: Baltimore-style

To make this block, refer to Lesson 9; in *Volume I*, Lessons 2, 8, and 10.

This vase of roses (three red, one prominently white) is a common pattern—in some form—in the Baltimore-style Album Quilts. In one block that I've seen, there were five red roses, but, again, one prominently central white one. While I don't know why, I feel there must be some significance beyond aesthetics for the white rose's presence. These blocks could be very fancy as indeed we've seen, but this one is exceptionally simple, honing the style to its basics. The pattern you'll see is very straightforward. But Heidi Chesley Sandberg has interpreted the block so richly, using prints to advantage and ruching the overblown roses. This latitude of interpretation, from straightforward red, white, and green to rich prints and textures, has got to be part of Baltimore's appeal to so many of us.

PATTERN #10: "Vase of Full-Blown Roses I"

Type: Baltimore-style

Baltimore Beauties Fabric Note: For a rich, textured look, make these roses out of the Ombré Leaves print in Turkey Red, Russet, or Baltimore Blue with Victoria Green for foliage. To make the roses, follow Lesson 1's instructions for Rolled and Gathered Strip Flowers, Method #3. Cut the Ombré print 1¼" wide, on the bias, using pinking shears. For speed, machine stitch to gather in a line ⅛" parallel to the fold. When gathered, the shading in this "rainbow print" fabric is particularly dramatic. Mark your background cloth with a 1¾" circle for each rose. Coil the gathered strip, overlapping it slightly from a fringe at the center to the outside of the circle. The dimensional appearance of the Baltimore Blue Ombré Leaf stripe is perfect for giving contour to this simple compote shape. Such realism is the style taught us by old Baltimore.

PATTERN #13: "Victorian Ribbon Basket with Wire Ribbon Roses"

Type: "Beyond"; Designed by the author

To make this block, in *Volume I*, Lessons 5 and 10.

How can something so richly Victorian looking be so fast and simple? I designed this block as a 1½ hour Houston Quilt Market class to show shopowners how to use the wonderful ribbons so readily available today. (The block uses double-faced satin ribbon and shaded French wire ribbon.) We had fun. And based on that experience, I'd estimate that if you had your block 'kit' all assembled, three hours would probably give you a fully prepared block all ready to sew. This block is not only easy, but its graphic strength makes it a wonderful home decor (pillow or framed picture) motif. If you assembled basted kits for several at once, each one would only take an evening to hand stitch into an exceptional gift.

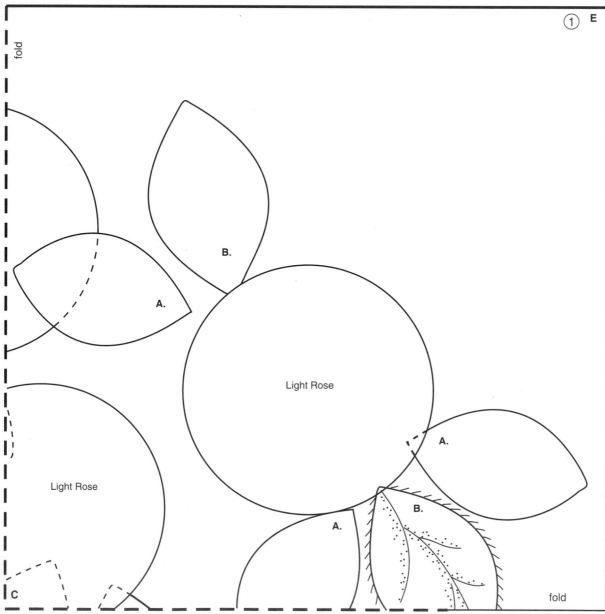

PATTERN #13: "Victorian Ribbon Basket with Wire Ribbon Roses"

Second page

Baltimore Beauties Fabric Note: Consider translating this ribbon block into cut cloth. I have made these roses with Lesson 1's Method #3: straight-tearing(intentionally fraying further) the gold Vermiculate and bias-cutting the red Ombré Leaves as described on Pattern #10. When you fold the strips wrong-side-in lengthwise, fold them ⅛" off-center to show a bit of the coloration of both the inside and the outside of the fabric. The Victoria Green Ombré Leaves print made into tucked leaves (Lesson 3) would enhance this block's character.

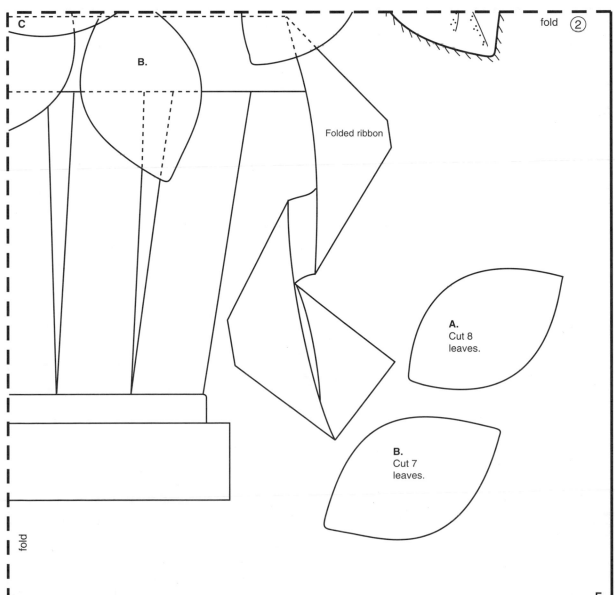

PATTERN #13: "Victorian Ribbon Basket with Wire Ribbon Roses"

Third page

To complete the Roses on the left half:
• Place two more roses and eight more leaves by eye.
• Each rose is 24" 1½"-wide shaded wired ribbon.
• The basket takes up to 2½ yds. of ⅝"- to 1"-wide ribbon.

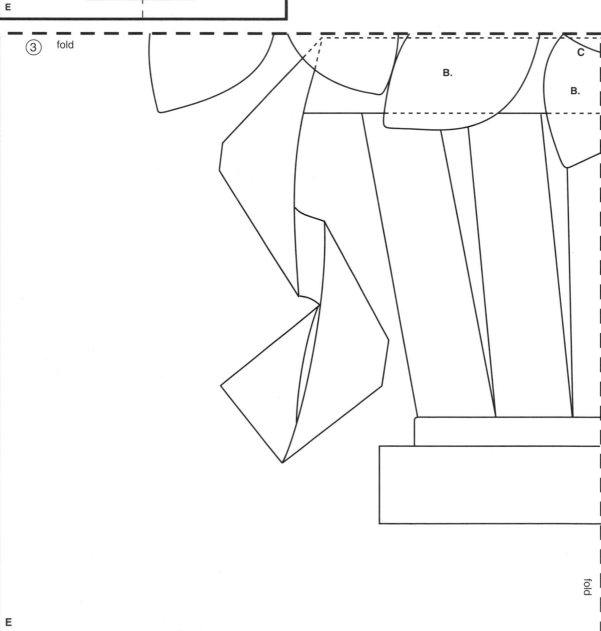

Pattern #13: "Victorian Ribbon Basket with Wire Ribbon Roses"

Fourth page

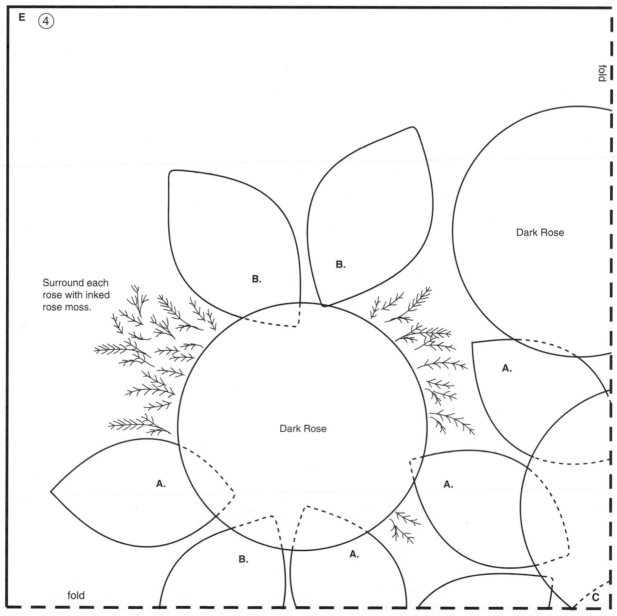

Surround each rose with inked rose moss.

fold

fold

B.

B.

Dark Rose

A.

A.

A.

A.

Dark Rose

B.

A.

C

PATTERN #23: "Texas Treasures"

Type: "Beyond"; Designed by J. Jane Mc. Mitchell

To make this block, refer to Lessons 4 and 6; in *Volume I*, Lessons 5, 9, and 10.

An Iris, Texas Bluebonnets, and the Yellow Rose of Texas all bloom from Jane's beautiful original design block. Taking inspiration from a traditional Baltimore pattern, Jane has made one of those blocks that seems simply perfect. The basket is a restrained weaving of three wine reds: a solid, a pindot, and a geometric. The flowers show close observation of nature. Their gestures are realistically appliquéd, and their characteristic details finely embroidered in sewing thread.

PATTERN #23: "Texas Treasures"

Second page

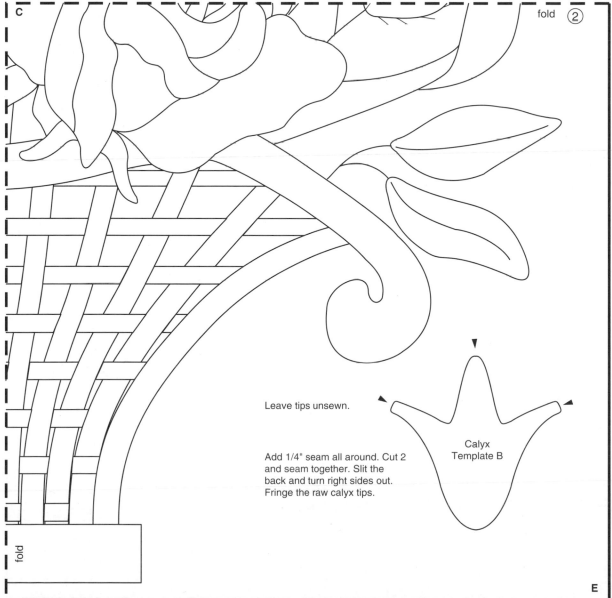

Leave tips unsewn.

Add 1/4" seam all around. Cut 2 and seam together. Slit the back and turn right sides out. Fringe the raw calyx tips.

Calyx
Template B

PATTERN #23: "Texas Treasures"

Third page

③ fold

C

E

Detail of Stem or Outline Stitch done
in single strand embroidery floss.

fold

E

PATTERN #23: "Texas Treasures"

Fourth page

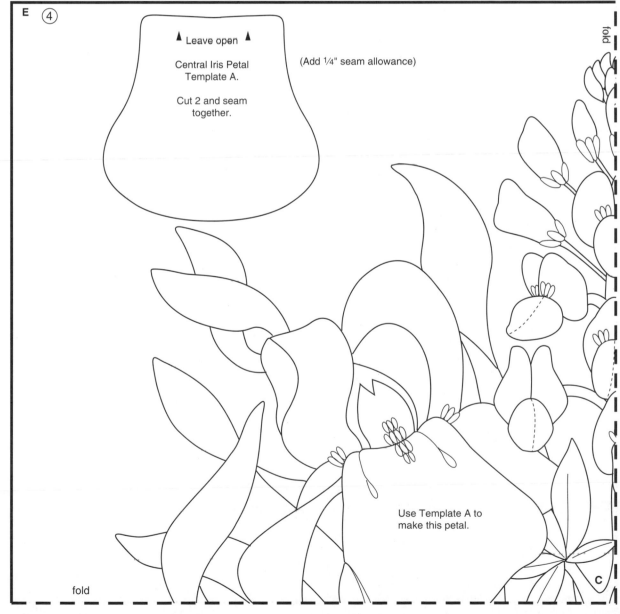

▲ Leave open ▲

Central Iris Petal
Template A.

Cut 2 and seam
together.

(Add ¼" seam allowance)

Use Template A to
make this petal.

fold

PATTERN #24A: "Fancy Flowers"

Type: "Beyond"; Designed by the author

To make this block, refer to Lessons 3, 8, 9; in *Volume I*, Lessons 6, 7, 8, 9, 10, and 11.

This ornate block was taught in a series article in *Quilter's Newsletter Magazine* and is the subject of Lesson 9. All of the techniques are covered either in this book's lessons, or in *Volume I*. The Key points to the techniques used, while the lessons where these methods appear are cited above. A second vase (pattern #24B) is shown with half of its pattern to cut on the fold (on page 161). This second vase is the one from that antique original, which inspired me to design and make this block. Use whichever vase you choose, and fill it full with the fancy flowers your heart desires.

PATTERN #24A: "Fancy Flowers"

Second page

Key to this block's techniques:

1. Superfine Stem Variation   **2.** *Broderie Perse* Leaf   **3.** Stuffed Silk Roses

4. Template-Free Flowers   **5.** Inked Embellishments

6. Thread Embellishments   **7.** Top-Stitching   **8.** Blanket-Stitching

9. Perfect Grapes   **10.** Ruched Flowers (Yellow Zinnias for "thoughts of absent friends")

11. Reverse Appliqué for tulip petals and cut-glass details on the Vase

12. Rick Rack Roses   **13.** Folded-Circle Rosebuds

PATTERN #24A: "Fancy Flowers"

Third page

fold

Detail: Stem or Outline Stitch done in
single strand embroidery floss

E

PATTERN #24A: "Fancy Flowers"

Fourth page

PATTERN #24B
Optional Vase

Place Pattern
on fold.

fold

E ④

E ④

C

fold

fold

② ⑧ ③ ⑪ ③ ① ⑩ ⑫

PATTERN #26: "Rita Kilstrom's Round Basket"

Type: "Beyond"; Designed by Rita Kilstrom

Quite bold and modern-looking, this basket has the mass needed to hold heavy ribbon flower blooms beautifully.

PATTERN #26

PATTERN #25: "Victorian Weave Basket"

Type: "Beyond"; By Carol Spalding

Patterns #25 through #33 are all contemporary basket patterns. To make these baskets, refer to Lessons 2 through 6; in *Volume I,* Lesson 9.

Carol has combined warps of pre-turned cotton bias stems with weavers of narrow silk "ribbon-floss" in an exquisite basket.

PATTERN #25

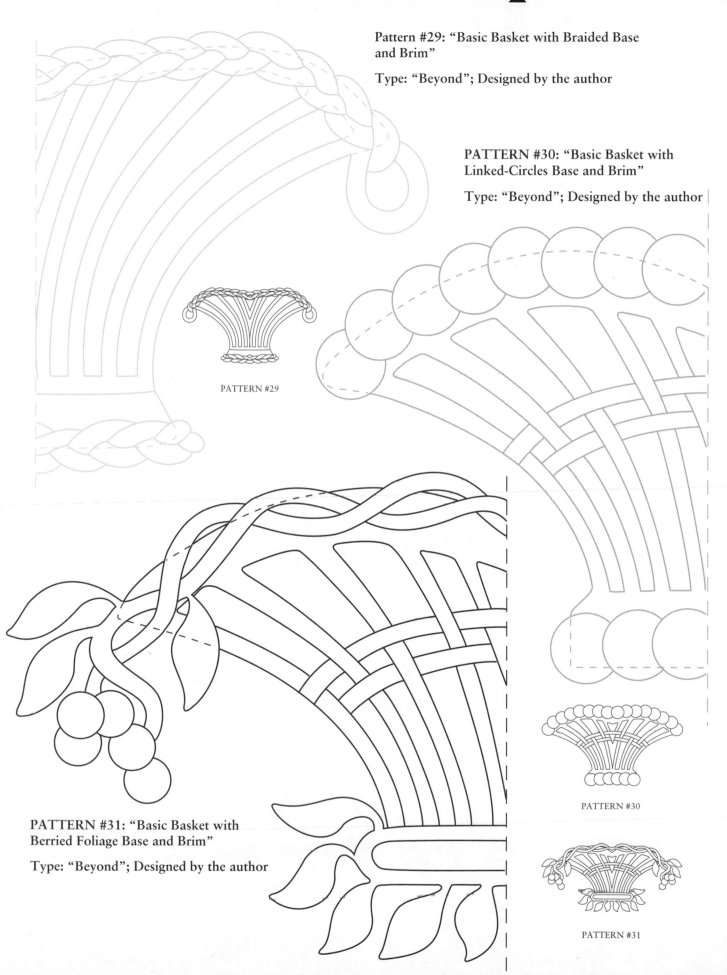

Pattern #29: "Basic Basket with Braided Base and Brim"

Type: "Beyond"; Designed by the author

PATTERN #30: "Basic Basket with Linked-Circles Base and Brim"

Type: "Beyond"; Designed by the author

PATTERN #29

PATTERN #31: "Basic Basket with Berried Foliage Base and Brim"

Type: "Beyond"; Designed by the author

PATTERN #30

PATTERN #31

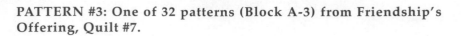

PATTERN #3: One of 32 patterns (Block A-3) from Friendship's Offering, Quilt #7.

Type: Beyond Baltimore

To make this block, refer to *Volume I*, Lesson 1 or 2.

PATTERN #4: One of 32 patterns (Block A-4) from Friendship's Offering, Quilt #7.

Type: Beyond Baltimore

To make this block, refer to *Volume I*, Lesson 1 or 2.

Patterns 3, 4, 11, 12, 13, 14, 21, 22, 25, and 26 are all from Quilt #7 in *Papercuts and Plenty*.

PATTERN #11: One of 32 patterns (Block B-5) from Friendship's Offering, Quilt #7.

Type: Beyond Baltimore

To make this block, refer to *Volume I*, Lesson 1 or 2.

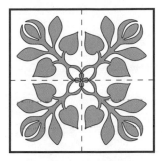

PATTERN #12: One of 32 patterns (Block B-6) from Friendship's Offering, Quilt #7.

Type: Beyond Baltimore

To make this block, refer to *Volume I*, Lesson 1 or 2.

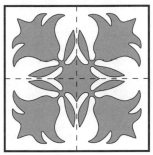

PATTERN #13: One of 32 patterns (Block C-2, Cabin Fever Calicoes) from Friendship's Offering, Quilt #7.

Type: Beyond Baltimore. Designed by the author.

To make this block, refer to *Volume I*, Lesson 1 or 2.

PATTERN #14: One of 32 patterns (Block C-5, Hearts and Hands) from Friendship's Offering, Quilt #7.

Type: Beyond Baltimore. Designed by the author.

To make this block, refer to *Volume 1*, Lesson 1 or 2. Cut template as a four-repeat pattern.

PATTERN #21: One of 32 patterns (Block E-1) from Friendship's Offering, Quilt #7.

Type: Beyond Baltimore

To make this block, refer to *Volume I*, Lesson 1 or 2.

PATTERN #22: One of 32 patterns (Block E-2, Cherubs) from Friendship's Offering, Quilt #7.

Type: Beyond Baltimore. Designed by the author.

To make this block, refer to *Volume I*, Lesson 1 or 2.

PATTERN #25: One of 32 patterns (Block E-5, Garden Cats) from Friendship's Offering, Quilt #7.

Type: Beyond Baltimore. Designed by the author.

To make this block, refer to *Volume I*, Lesson 1 or 2.

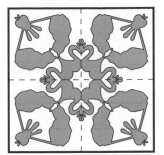

PATTERN #26: One of 32 patterns (Block E-6) from Friendship's Offering, Quilt #7.

Type: Beyond Baltimore

To make this block, refer to *Volume I*, Lesson 1 or 2.

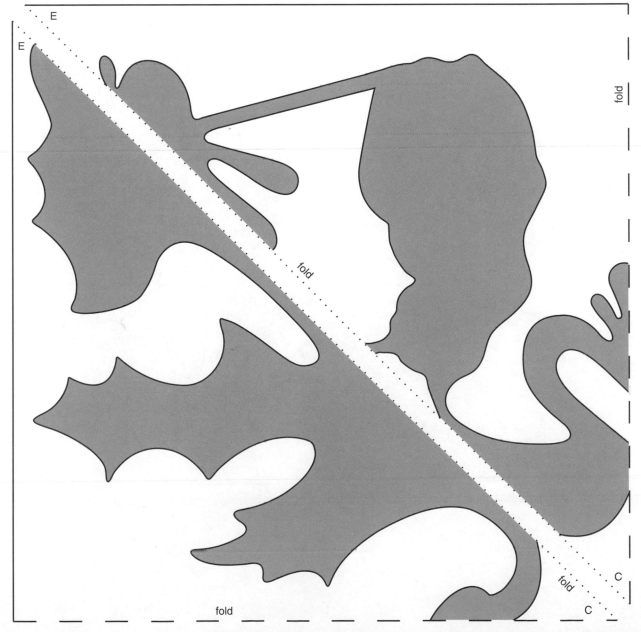

PATTERN #33: One of 29 patterns (Block A-1, Simpler Palmetto Frame) from Classic Revival: Alex's Album.

Type: Classic Baltimore

To make this block, refer to *Volume I*, Lesson 1 or 2.

PATTERN #34: One of 29 patterns (Block A-2, Botanical Variation) from Classic Revival: Alex's Album, Quilt #6.

Type: Baltimore-Style

To make this block, refer to *Volume I*, Lesson 1 or 2.
Patterns 33, 34, 37, 38, 41, 42, 43, 44, 46, 51, 52, 55, and 56 are from Quilt #6 in *Papercuts and Plenty*.

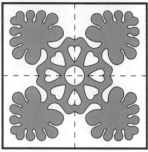

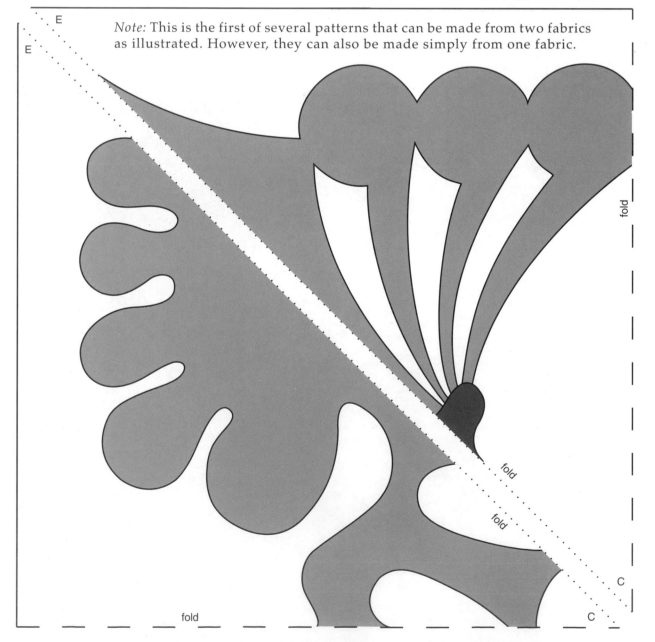

Note: This is the first of several patterns that can be made from two fabrics as illustrated. However, they can also be made simply from one fabric.

PATTERN #37: One of 29 patterns (Block B-2, Fleur-de-Lis and Rose Medallion) from Classic Revival: Alex's Album, Quilt #6.

Type: Beyond Baltimore

To make this block, refer to *Volume I*, Lesson 1 or 2.

PATTERN #38: One of 29 patterns (Block B-3, George Washington's Redbud) from Classic Revival: Alex's Album, Quilt #6.

Type: Beyond Baltimore. Designed by the author.

To make this block, refer to *Volume I*, Lesson 1 or 2.

PATTERN #41: One of 29 patterns (Block C-2, Sunflower) from Classic Revival: Alex's Album, Quilt #6.

Type: Classic Baltimore, from the Album inscribed "Seidenstricker," "Baltimore," and "1845."

To make this block, refer to *Volume I*, Lesson 1 or 2.

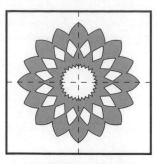

PATTERN #42: One of 29 patterns (Block C-3, Palmetto Border) from Classic Revival: Alex's Album, Quilt #6. This pattern contains silhouette portraits by the author and is repeated in blocks E-2, E-3, E-4, and G-3. The ink portraits were done by Technique #2, which is taught on pages 22–23 in *Volume II*.

Type: Classic Baltimore, from the Album inscribed "Seidenstricker," "Baltimore," and "1845."

To make this block, refer to *Volume I*, Lesson 1 or 2.

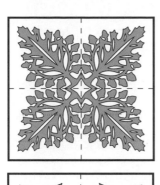

PATTERN #43: One of 29 patterns (Block C-4, Oak Leaves and Acorns—for Longevity) from Classic Revival: Alex's Album, Quilt #6.

Type: Beyond Baltimore. Designed by the author.

To make this block, refer to *Volume I*, Lesson 1 or 2.

PATTERN #44: One of 29 patterns (Block C-5, Sweet Gum for the Severn River) from Classic Revival: Alex's Album, Quilt #6.

Type: Beyond Baltimore. Designed by the author.

To make this block, refer to *Volume I*, Lesson 1 or 2.

PATTERN #46: One of 29 patterns (Block D-2, *E Pluribus Unum*: Eagles and Oaks) from Classic Revival: Alex's Album, Quilt #6.

Type: Beyond Baltimore. Designed by the author.

To make this block, refer to *Volume I*, Lesson 1 or 2. For the eagle's feathers, slash to the inside corner's turn line, following the method for Dogtooth Borders taught on page 78 in *Volume II*. Cut the freezer paper template for this pattern as a four-repeat.

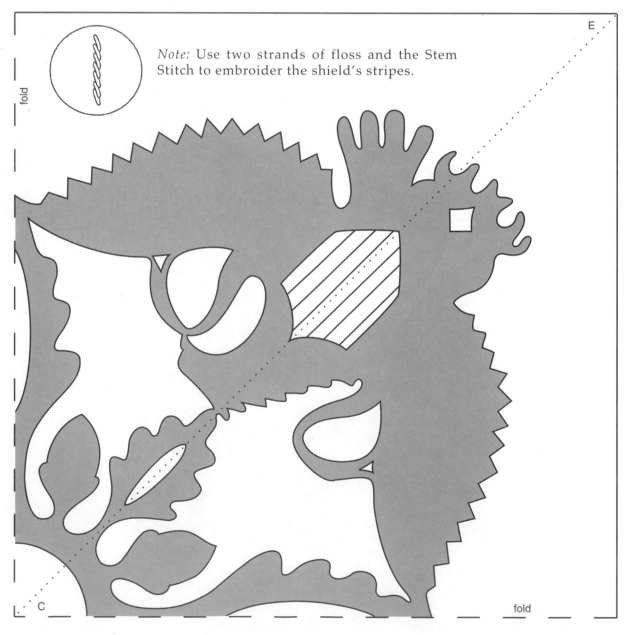

Note: Use two strands of floss and the Stem Stitch to embroider the shield's stripes.

PATTERN #51: One of 29 patterns (Block F-3, Devon Violets for Nana) from Classic Revival: Alex's Album, Quilt #6.

Type: Beyond Baltimore. Designed by the author.

To make this block, refer to *Volume I*, Lesson 1 or 2.

PATTERN #52: One of 29 patterns (Block F-4, Flowers Around Friendship's Chain) from Classic Revival: Alex's Album, Quilt #6.

Type: Beyond Baltimore. Designed by the author.

To make this block, refer to *Volume I*, Lesson 1 or 2.

PATTERN #55: One of 29 patterns (Block G-4, Ring with Holly) from Classic Revival: Alex's Album, Quilt #6.

Type: Baltimore-Style

To make this block, refer to *Volume I*, Lesson 1 or 2.

PATTERN #56: One of 29 patterns (Block G-5, Botanical Variation in Honor of Victoria Jean McKibben Hamilton) from Classic Revival: Alex's Album, Quilt #6.

Type: Beyond Baltimore. Designed by the author.

To make this block, refer to *Volume I*, Lesson 1 or 2.

PATTERN #72: Vase of Full-Blown Roses II: Rose Amphora.

Type: Baltimore-Style

To make this block, refer in *Volume I*, to Lesson 10.

This faithfully reproduced block was first pictured as Color Plate #1 in *Volume I*, but no pattern accompanied it there.

Note: This pattern's embroidery is optional. The leaves can be stitched with a single strand of machine embroidery thread using the Stem or Outline Stitch. The rose moss can be embroidered in the Fly stitch with a single strand of silk sewing thread. These embellishiment details can also be drawn with a Pigma pen.

PATTERN #72: Vase of Full-Blown Roses II: Rose Amphora.

Second page

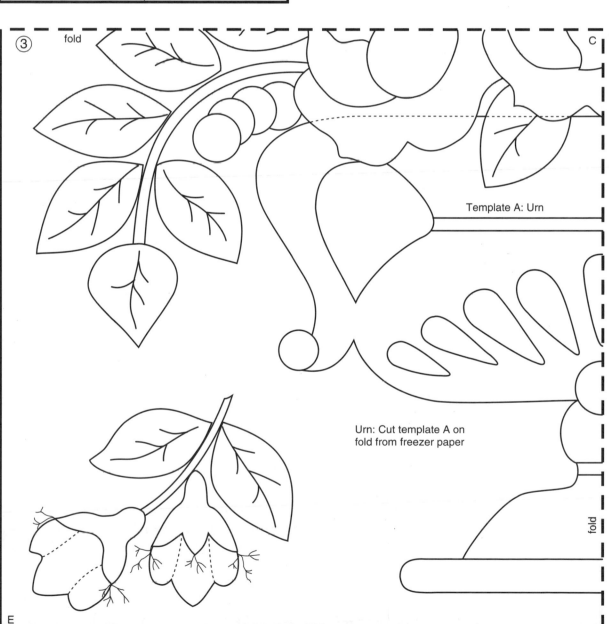

PATTERN #72: Vase of Full-Blown Roses II: Rose Amphora.

Third page

Template A: Urn

Urn: Cut template A on
fold from freezer paper

fold

PATTERN #72: Vase of Full-Blown Roses II: Rose Amphora.

Fourth page

PATTERN #76: Tree of Life.

Type: Baltimore-Style. (Block F-5 from the Metropolitan Museum of Art's Album Quilt, Photo 26 in *Volume I*)

To make this block, refer to *Volume I*, Lessons 2 and 10.

The Tree of Life is an ancient symbol going far back to early civilizations. It seemed we couldn't finish our Album Quilt series without including a pattern for this classic Album block. A color version of this block is pictured in the East Bay Heritage Quilters' Album, Quilt #14 in *Volume II*.

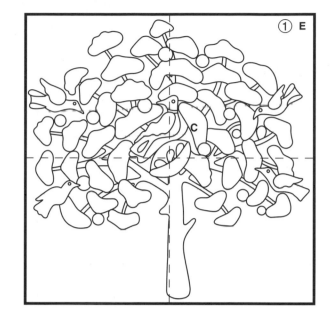

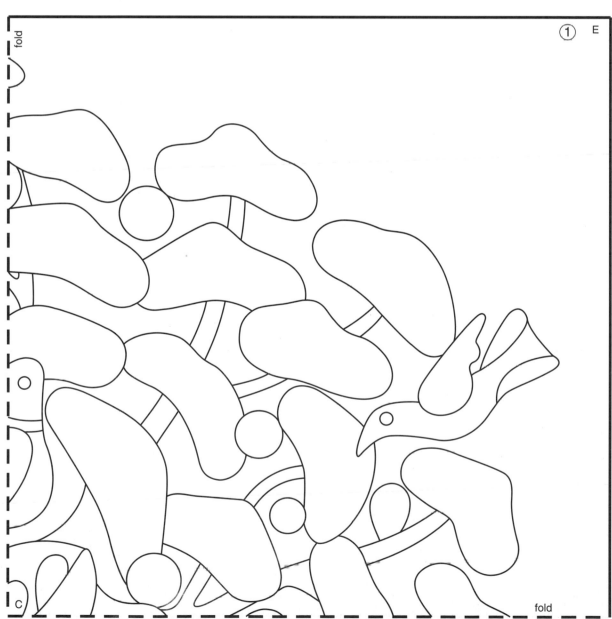

PATTERN #76: Tree of Life.

Second page

PATTERN #76: Tree of Life.

Third page

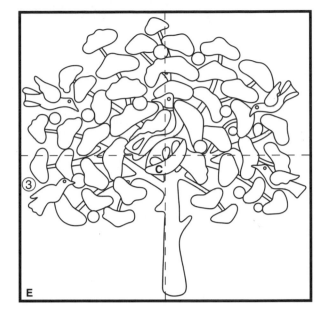

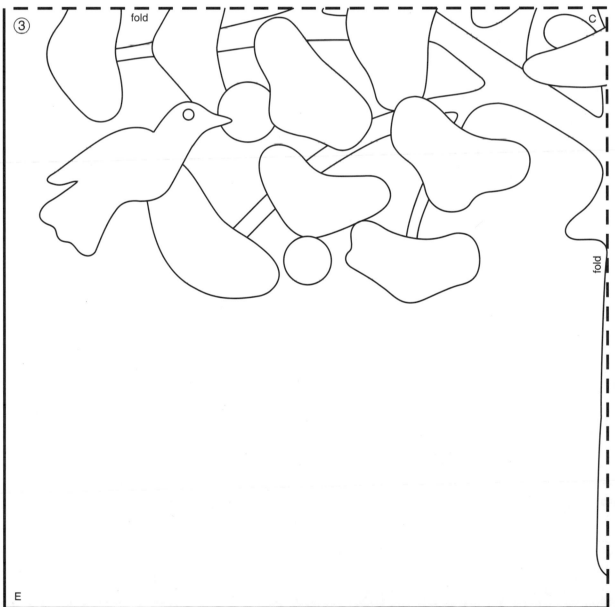

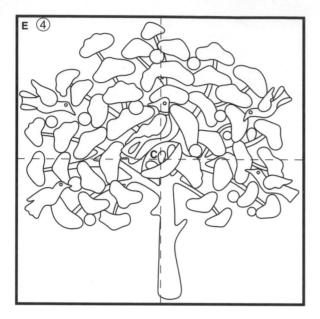

PATTERN #76: Tree of Life.

Fourth page

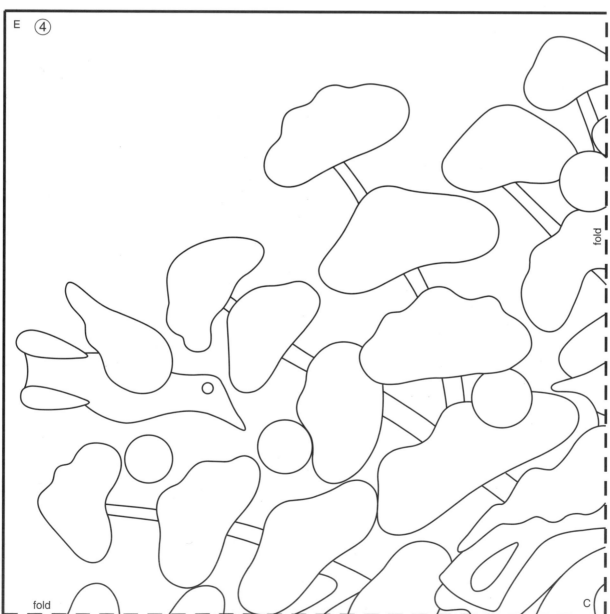

PATTERN #79: Geranium Bird.

Type: Baltimore-Style

To make this block, refer to *Volume I*, Lessons 2, 5, 9, and 10.

This pattern is by an antebellum needleartist whom I've dubbed "The Whimsical Botanist." Her hand seems distinctive in some or all of the blocks in Quilt #6 in *Dimensional Appliqué.* Marjo Hodges did this book's charming replica of this block. She made perfect tiny yellow circle centers in the flowers, chain-stitched their fine stems, and came up with a clever solution to the wee buds: She machine-seamed (using a tiny stitch) a 1" x 12" strip of

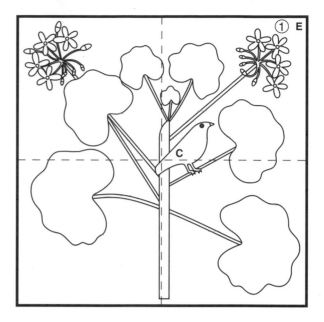

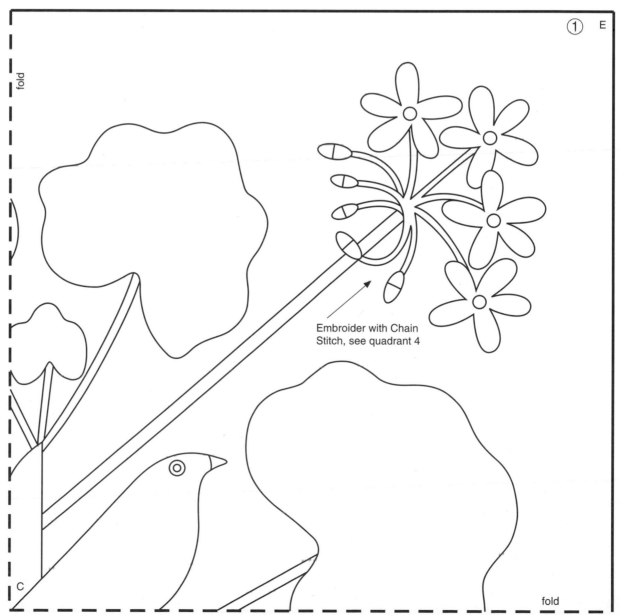

Embroider with Chain Stitch, see quadrant 4

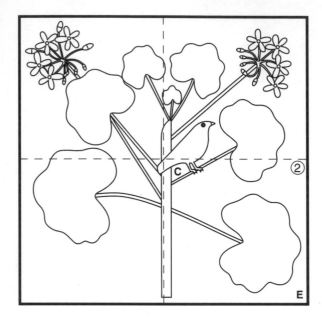

PATTERN #79: Geranium Bird.

Second page

red, right sides together with a same-size strip of green. Her seam was ⅛", trimmed back to ¹⁄₁₆" and pressed open after machining. Out of this red/green strip, she cut the buds, which were drawn with the appliqué seam allowance added on. From the collared look of the center stem-tip, to the straight-jutting leaf and flower stems, this block shows the quintessential geranium. No wonder this bird looks so content here! Another tree-perched bird in this

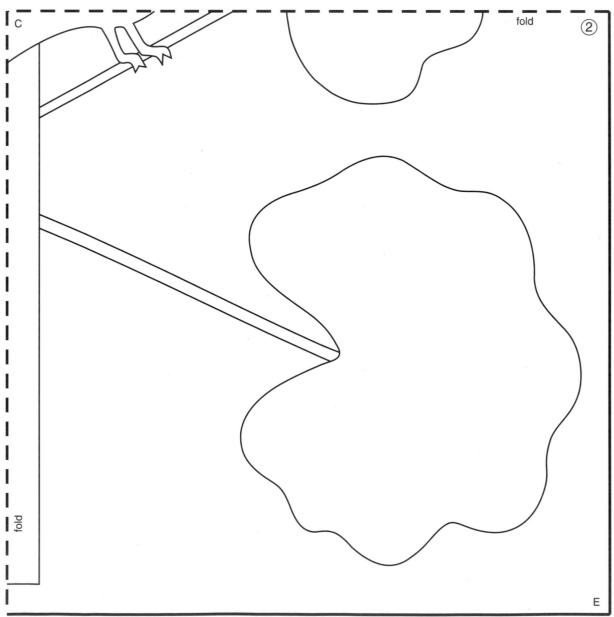

PATTERN #79: Geranium Bird.

Third page

same quilt has wee embroidered words, as if in song, coming from its beak. Unfortunately, I saw it hung at the Museum of American Art in Washington, D. C. It was protected there by an electronic "fence," which set off an alarm each time I craned upwards to try to read the words! But the idea is delightful: sweet messages sung to posterity by an appliquéd warbler.

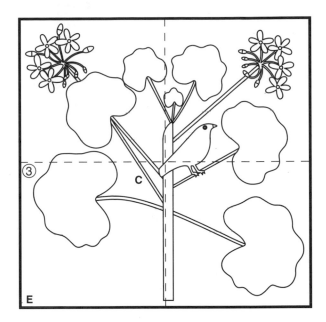

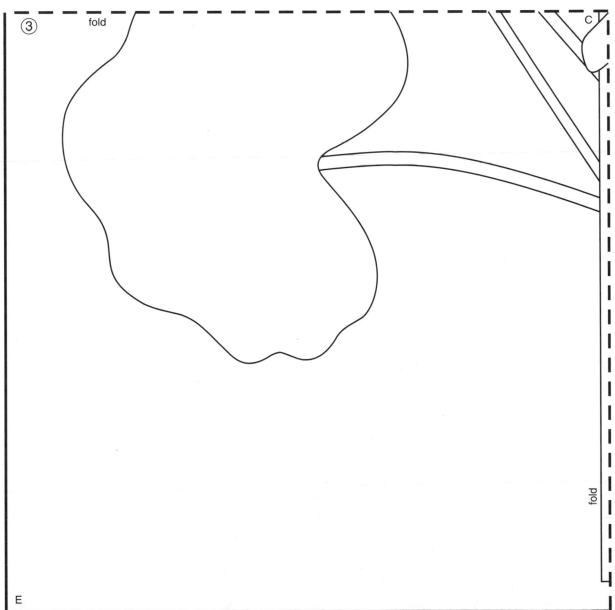

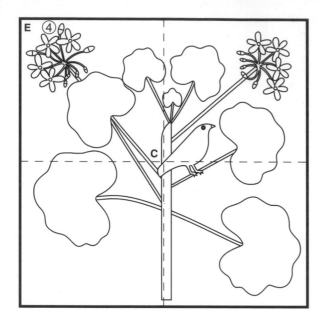

PATTERN #79: Geranium Bird.

Fourth page

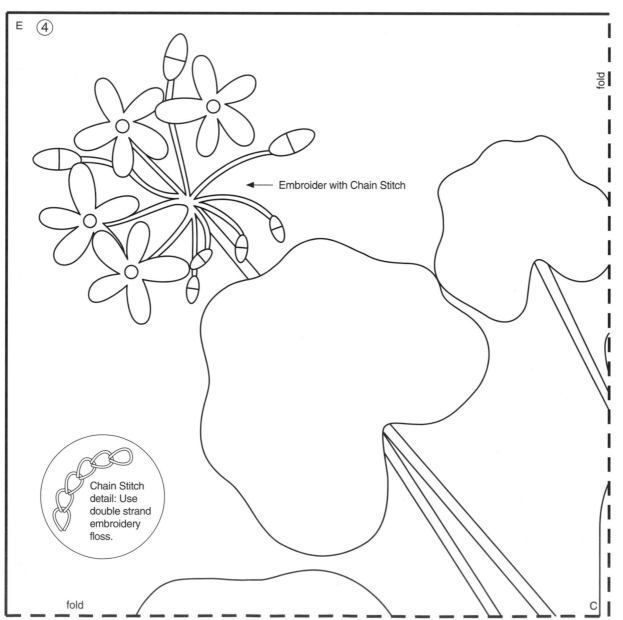

← Embroider with Chain Stitch

Chain Stitch detail: Use double strand embroidery floss.

E ④

fold

fold

C

PATTERN #81: Love Birds on a Rose Perch.

Type: Baltimore-Style

To make this block, refer to *Volume I*, Lessons 5, 7, 9, or 10.

These roses are stuffed and quilted ones taught in *Dimensional Appliqué's* Lesson 7. Here, Barbara Hain stitched these roses in three pieces: First she appliquéd, stuffed, then quilted the tight inner petals of polished red cotton at the rose's top. Next she applied a sprigged yellow print center and appliquéd the large red lower rose petals. When the rose was fully stuffed, she closed the opening left in its base and quilted its petals.

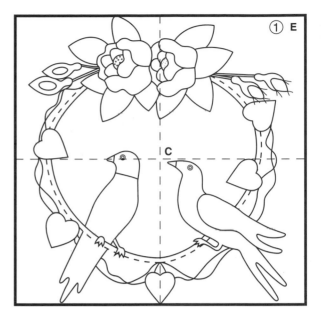

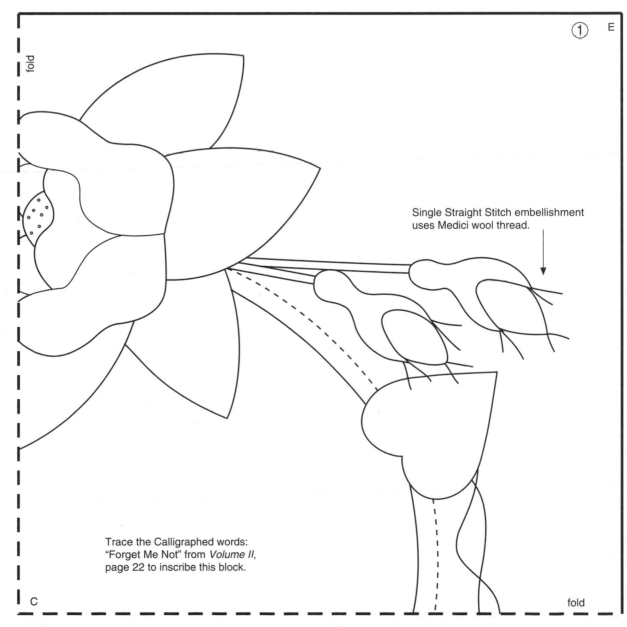

Single Straight Stitch embellishment uses Medici wool thread.

Trace the Calligraphed words: "Forget Me Not" from *Volume II*, page 22 to inscribe this block.

fold

C

fold

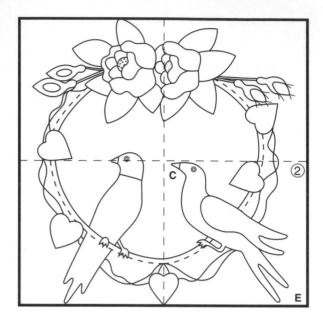

PATTERN #81: Love Birds on a Rose Perch.

Second page

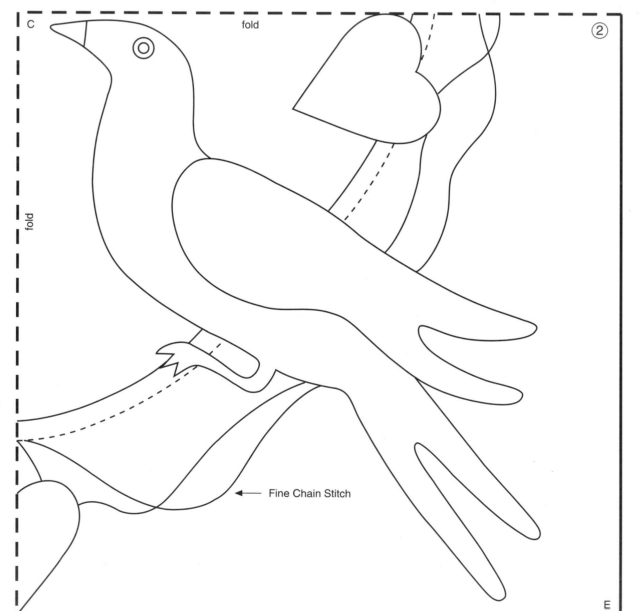

Fine Chain Stitch

PATTERN #81: Love Birds on a Rose Perch.

Third page

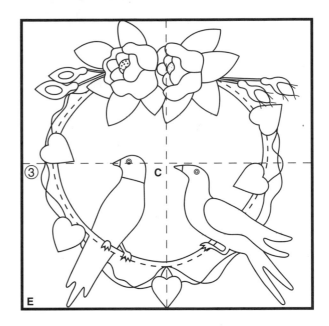

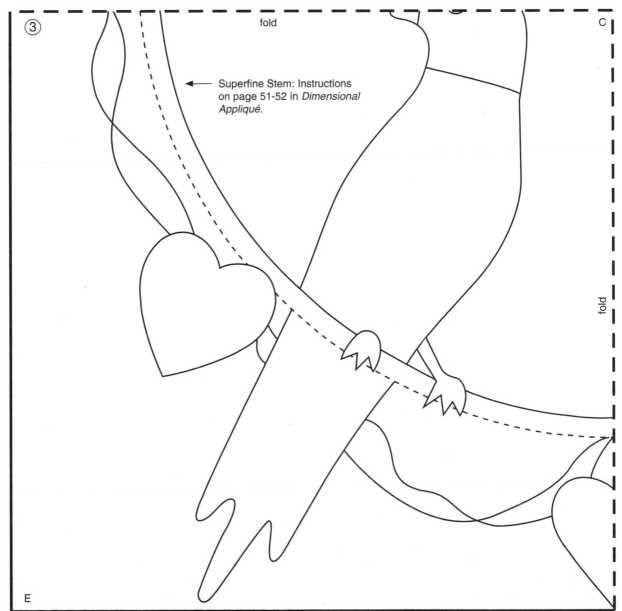

◄— Superfine Stem: Instructions on page 51-52 in *Dimensional Appliqué.*

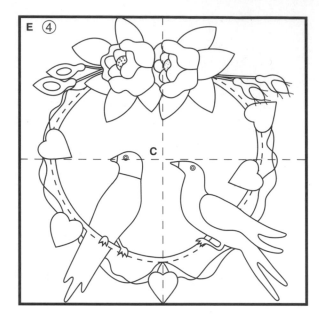

PATTERN #81: Love Birds on a Rose Perch.

Fourth page

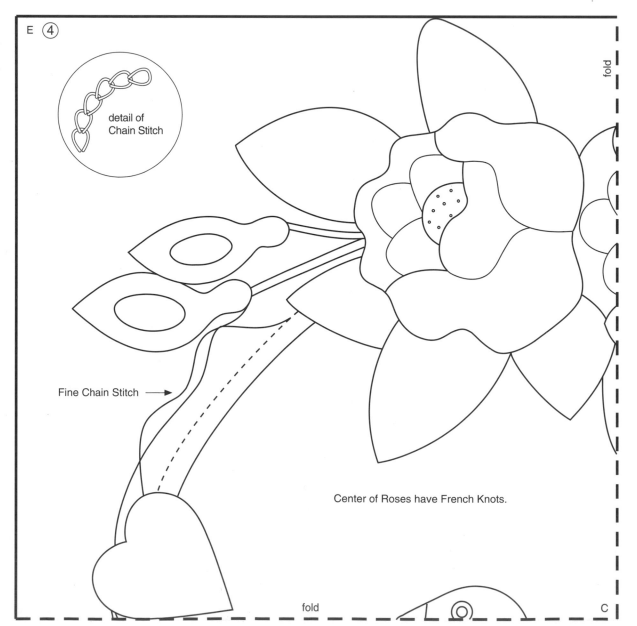

detail of Chain Stitch

Fine Chain Stitch →

Center of Roses have French Knots.

fold

E ④

C

PATTERN #84: Epergne of Fruit III.

Type: Classic Baltimore

To make this block, refer to Lessons 1 and 2, and in *Volume I*, Lessons 5, 7, 9, or 10.

Technology and ideology may both beam from this elegant display of fruit. The Industrial Revolution swelled the ranks of the middle class and brought them new wealth. Decorative style on all fronts was diverse and in rapid transition. Though some of the changes might seem to us to be small details, for the middle-class homemaker, they were exciting opportunities for self-expression. In glassmaking for example, the 1830s ushered in the new technique of pressed glass. In

PATTERN #84: Epergne of Fruit III.

Second page

tableware, compotes, and epergnes, those neo-classical raised-glass dishes, which show off fruits as beautifully as a vase does flowers, made an *au courant* fashion statement. Often this glassware is stitched into the Albums in the cerulean or indigo blue we identify with Baltimore: Blue was a symbolic color, the color of truth and the soul.

A prime Odd Fellow symbol is the cornucopia overflowing with the bounty and the blessings of this earth. In the baskets and bowls of fruits, we probably see the same gratitude expressed. Perhaps this was a modi-

PATTERN #84: Epergne of Fruit III.

Third page

fication dear to the Rebekahs. Or perhaps the symbolism was so apparent all would understand these variants. Clear delight seems to have been taken in depicting fruits and flowers with realistic touches (evidence of the beatitude of closely observing God's plan).

Cut epergne double on fold. ⟶

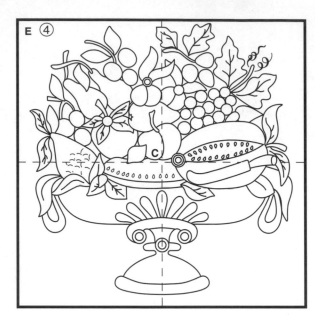

PATTERN #84: Epergne of Fruit III.

Fourth page

PATTERN #85: Epergne of Fruit IV.

Type: Classic Baltimore. (From a Numsen family quilt shown in *Stitched in Cloth, Carved in Stone,* the sequel to *Volume III*)

To make this block, refer to Lessons 1 and 2, and in *Volume I*, Lessons 5, 7, 9, or 10.

Wendy Grande drafted this pattern from a picture of one of the Numsen Family Quilts. She was inspired to experiment with gauging, an old and little-known needlework technique, which involves a systematic shrinking of a shape from a larger to a smaller size by shirring its fabric.

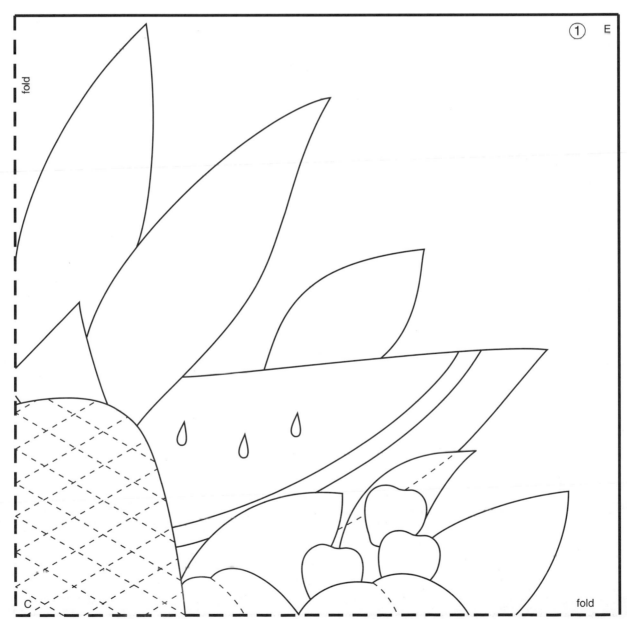

PATTERN #85: Epergne of Fruit IV.

Second page

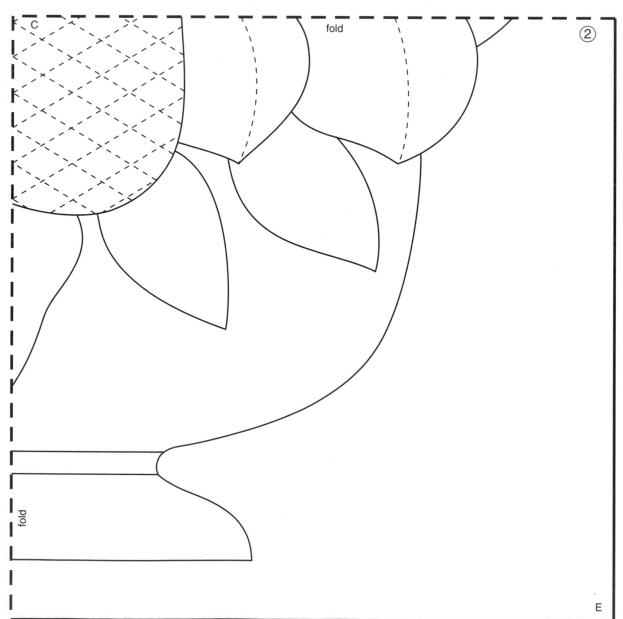

PATTERN #85: Epergne of Fruit IV.

Third page

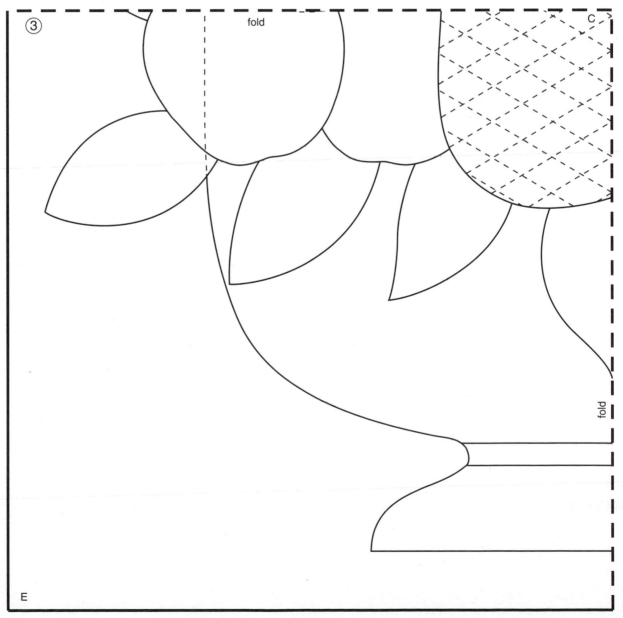

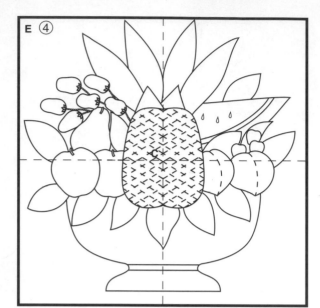

PATTERN #85: Epergne of Fruit IV.

Fourth page

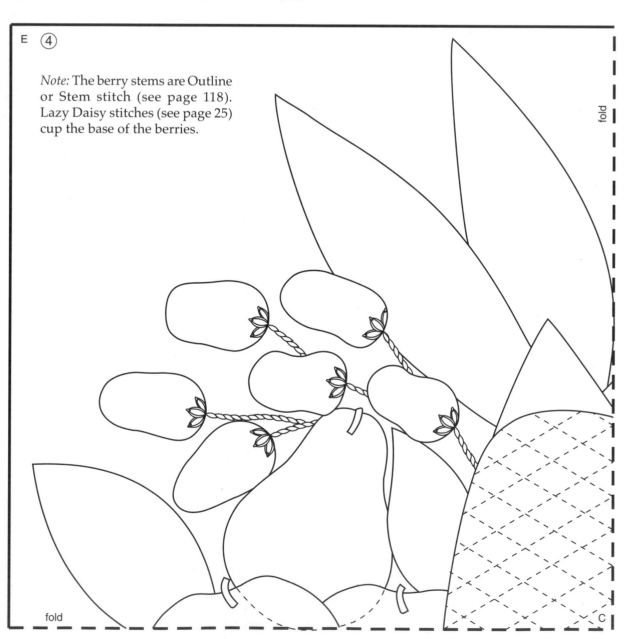

Note: The berry stems are Outline or Stem stitch (see page 118). Lazy Daisy stitches (see page 25) cup the base of the berries.

PATTERN #1: "Crown of Laurel with Rose"

Type: Baltimore-style designed by the author

This block was inspired by a memorial found in the graveyard of the First Presbyterian Church, King's Highway, Lewes, Delaware.

Procedure

1. Fold the 16" print background square into quarters and fingerpress the creases.
2. Feature the right or wrong side of the print. With a pencil or Pigma .01 pen in brown, lightly mark the left and right inner and outer circle line and the rose. (Be careful not to mark full circle.)
3. Make the ribbon boat leaves, pinning them in layers from the bottom of the wreath to the top so the upper leaves overlap the lower. Place the outer leaves first, then middle, then inner, so the leaves

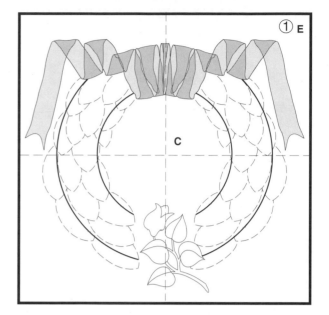

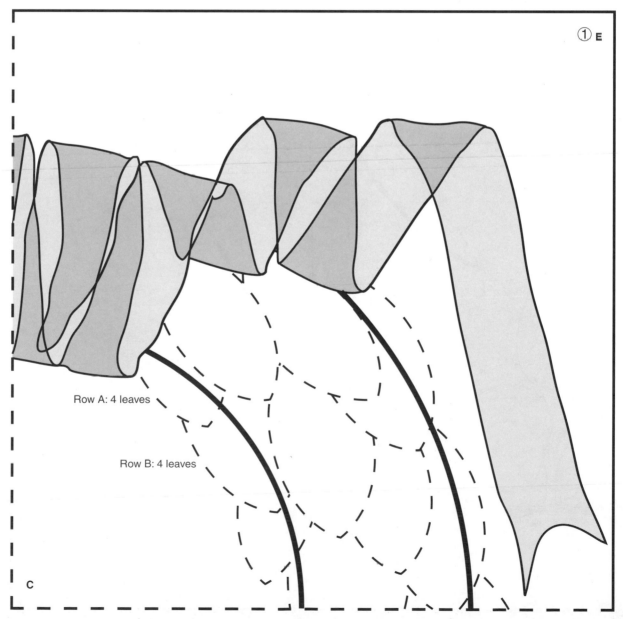

Row A: 4 leaves

Row B: 4 leaves

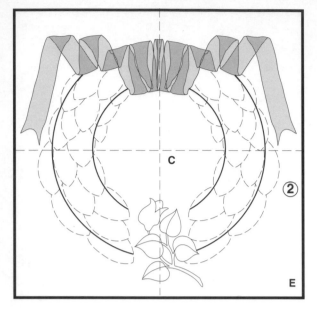

PATTERN #1: "Crown of Laurel with Rose"

Second Page

overlap from inside to outside. Baste, then appliqué the leaves in place by tack or stab stitch.

4. Use a Pigma Micron .01 pen and a penny to draw the berries ½" apart on 1" wide ribbon. Cut, adding ⅛" seam allowance all around. Seal the cut edges with clear nail polish. "Hem under" the seam allowance, using a running stitch just inside the folded edge. The folded edge should be the inked circle. Pull the thread to gather into a cup. Make a spit ball from a 1" x 2" strip of paper towel. Gather the ball and blind stitch it to wreath.

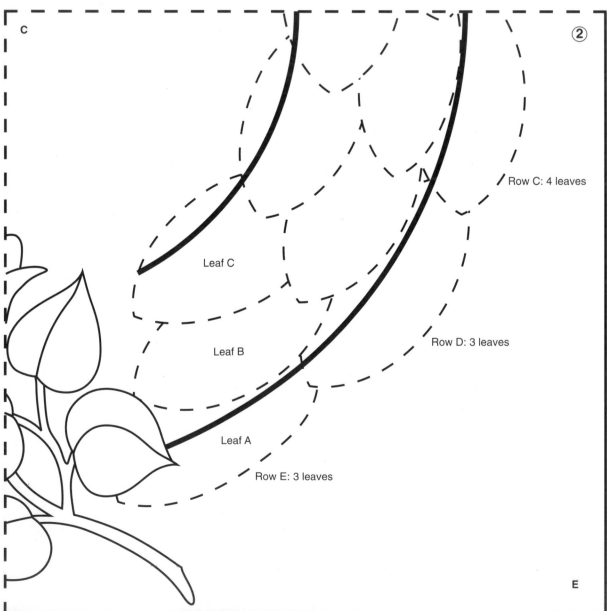

PATTERN #1: "Crown of Laurel with Rose"

Third Page

5. Go over the rose placement lines in Pigma pen so the leaf outlines can be seen from the back. From the wrong side (the back) pin two 2" green squares over these "show through" text outlines. Appliqué the rose leaves in place with running stitches taken from the back, through the drawn lines. If you prefer, mark the leaves on the front and stitch from the front. Trim the excess off from the front in either method.

6. Stem Stitch the rose stems and center veins. Top stitch the leaves.

7. Make the rosebud as on page 111 in *Romancing Ribbons*. Embroider the rose moss with back-to-back blanket stitches.

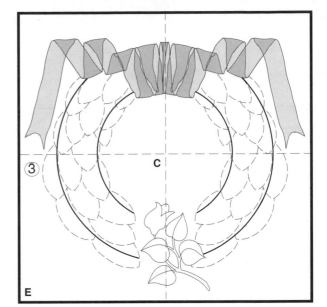

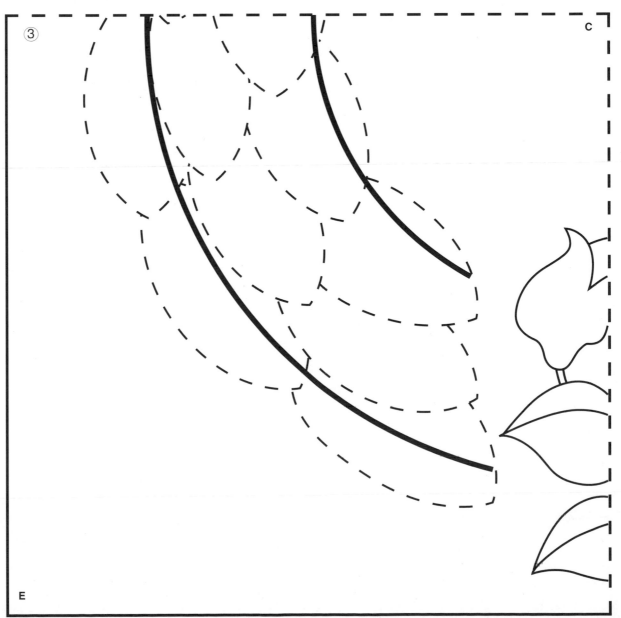

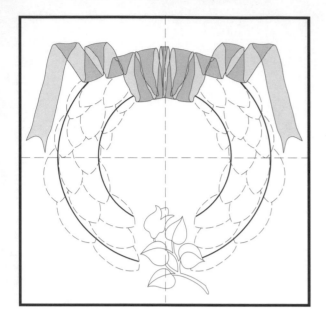

PATTERN #1: "Crown of Laurel with Rose"

Fourth Page

8. Make the rose calyx. You can cut double layer, raw edged as with #5 above.

LEAVES from French Shaded Wired Ribbon

Row A: (Topmost Row):4 leaves on the left, 4 leaves on the right=8 leaves of size **3** x 6". Make 8 leaves from one 48" length of ⅝"-wide size **3** ribbon. (CID [Creative Import Designs] style #1359, color 3) Cut 8 leaves 6" long each. Fold each 6" ribbon length in half—raw edge on top of raw edge—and sew a boat shape. Optional: Seam the dark edge of three leaves, the light edge of one leaf.

Row B: 4 leaves on the left, 4 leaves on the right=8 leaves of size **5** x 4". Make 8 leaves from one 32" length of ⅞" wide size **5** ribbon. (CID style #534, color 239) Fold each 6" ribbon length in half from bottom to top—wire edge on top of wire edge—and sew a boat shape.

Row C: 4 leaves on the left, 4 leaves on the right=8 leaves of size **9** x 4.5". Make 8 leaves from one 36" length of 1½" wide size **9** ribbon. (CID style #534, color 238) Fold each 4½" ribbon length in half—wire edge on top of wire edge—and sew a boat shape.

Row D: 3 leaves on the left, 3 leaves on the right=6 leaves of size **5** x 8". Make 6 leaves from one 48" length of ⅞" wide size **5** ribbon. (CID style #1359, color 3) Cut 6 leaves at 8" long. Fold each 8" ribbon length in half—raw edge on top of raw edge—from right to left and sew a boat shape along the light edge.

Row E (Bottom Row): 3 leaves on the left, 3 leaves on the right=6 leaves of size **5** x 8". Make 6 leaves from one 48" length of ⅞" wide size **5** ribbon. (CID style #930, color 889) Fold each 8" ribbon length in half—raw edges together—from right to left and sew a boat shape.

Rose Branchlet: 5" scrap of green calico

Rose bud: size **9**; a 1½" x 4½" length (CID style #534, color 235)

Berries from French Shaded Wired Ribbon: ⅞" (size **5**) or size **9** x 6". Use a 12" length for bud and berries.

Bow that ties the crown: Mokuba #1520 gold-edged organdy ribbon 55" long, color 49, 25 mm wide

DMC Pearl cotton size 5 floss in 3 shades of yellow green

PATTERN #2: "Bread and Wine within Border Frame"

Type: Baltimore-style designed by the author

To make this block (pictured on the back cover), refer to *Volume I*, Lesson 1, and refer to *Fancy Appliqué* for instruction on oil stenciling and UltraSuede appliqué.

The frame border is adapted from the Hunting Scene in *Spoken Without a Word*. To change from a 12½" square to a rectangle, use the triangular insert. 'Bread and Wine' was made by the author and Mary Sue Hannan to celebrate her brother-in-law ArchBishop Hannan's 60th year of priesthood. The frame and grapes are UltraSuede®. The grapes and challice are shaded with Craypas 'Specialist' Oil Pastels.

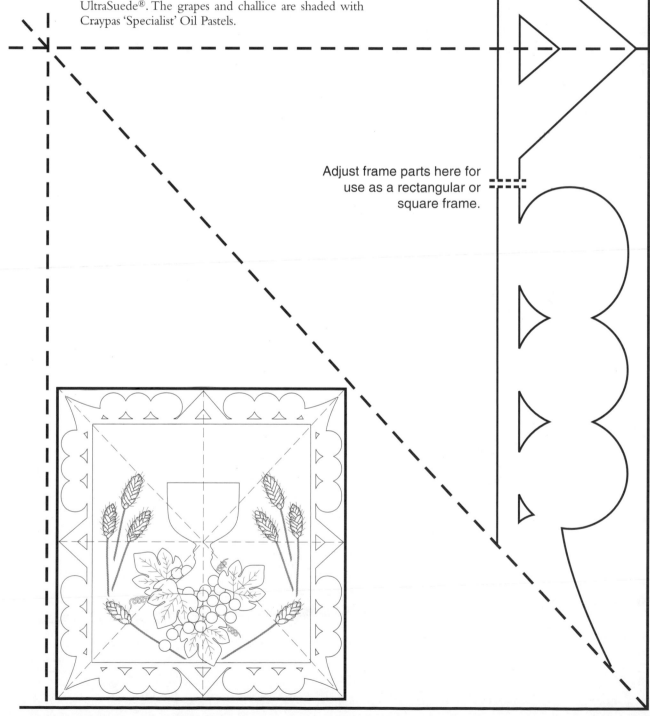

Adjust frame parts here for use as a rectangular or square frame.

E ④   ① E

PATTERN #2: "Bread and Wine within Border Frame"

Second Page

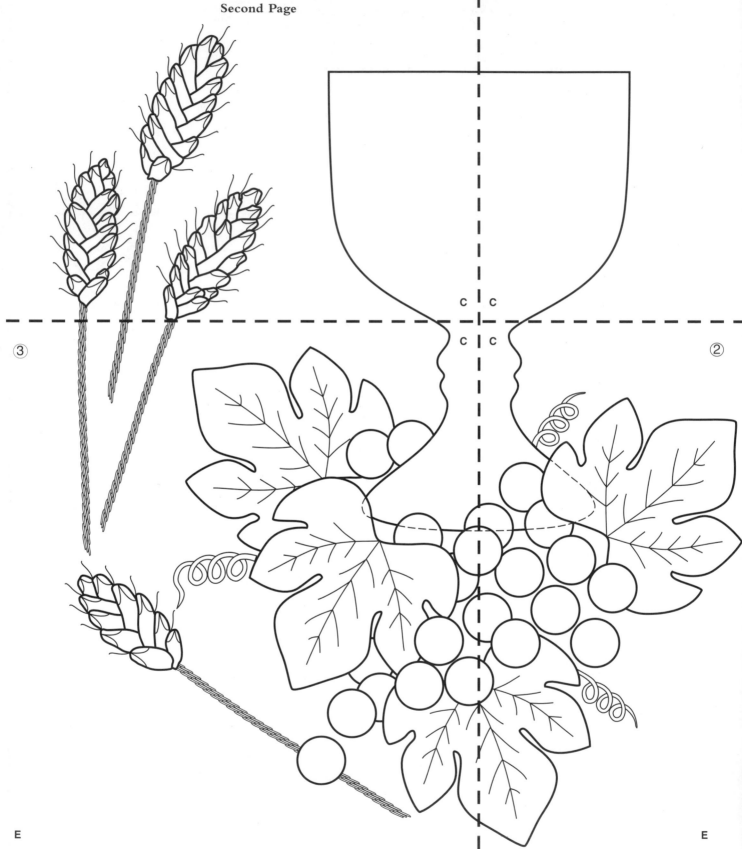

③   ②

E   E

PATTERN #3: "Patriotic Eagle"

Type: Classic Baltimore

To make this block, refer to *Volume I*, Lesson 12.

Replete with symbolism, this block with flag and eagle motifs is the center of an 1847-1850 quilt. There are several eagle blocks similar to this one in antique Albums. This one has a freedom or "liberty cap" on the flag staff, others do not. In Roman times the Phrygian cap, like this, was worn by freed slaves. It topped staves when French revolutionaries stormed the Bastille, and I theorize that the presence of this "striped cap" image in antebellum Baltimore Albums may witness the quiltmaker's abolitionist sentiments. Might cornucopias (striped in the Odd Fellows' red, yellow, and blue) also carry this connotation?

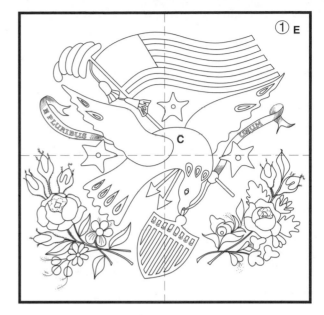

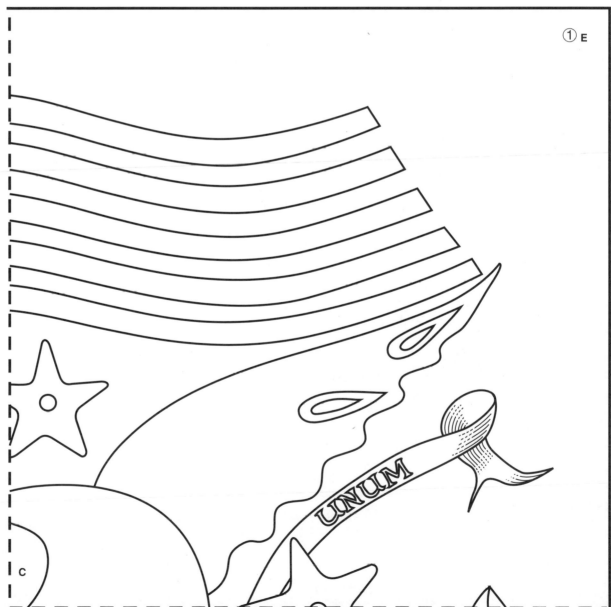

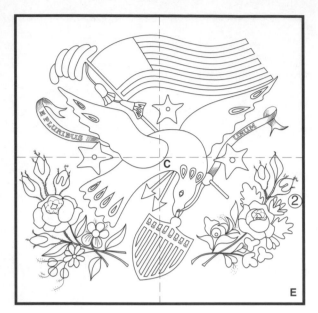

PATTERN #3: "Patriotic Eagle"

Second Page

PATTERN #3: "Patriotic Eagle"

Third Page

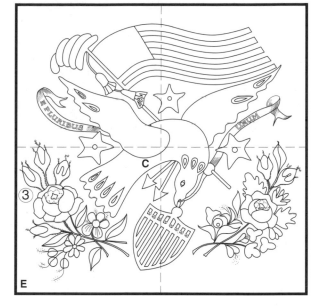

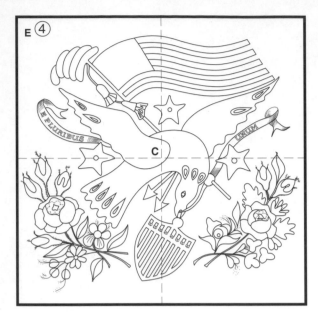

PATTERN #3: "Patriotic Eagle"

Fourth Page

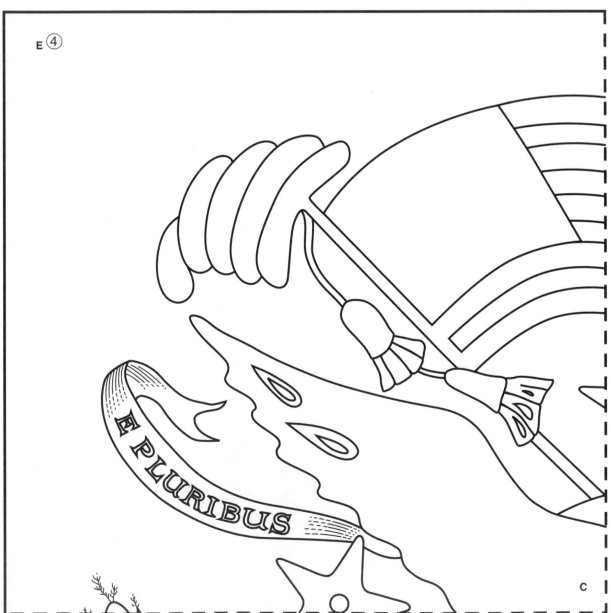

PATTERN #4: "Basket of Flowers"

Type: Classic Baltimore

To make this block (pictured on the back cover), refer to *Volume I*, Lesson 12 and *Romancing Ribbons into Flowers*, pages 111-16.

Since I first met the Baltimores, I have loved this simple, charming, clearly Victorian basket. Acorns (symbolic of immortality and longevity) nestle among the stems! It is from a quilt made for the Rev. Dr. Roberts in 1847-48 and is in the Lovely Lane Museum, Baltimore. The Beyond Baltimore version on the back cover is one I made. The basket is reverse appliquéd cotton, the stems are 4mm silk embroidery ribbon, pierced leaf stitched. The leaves are both cotton and ribbon appliqué. The blooms and buds are shaded wired ribbon, the calyxes are UltraSuede®.

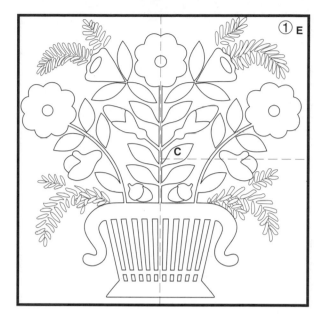

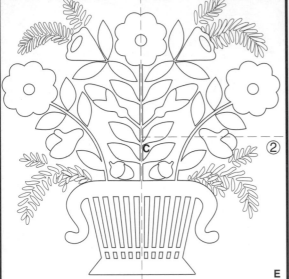

PATTERN #4: "Basket of Flowers"

Second Page

Measurements and ribbon sizes for replicating the version pictured are on pages 112-116 in *Romancing Ribbons.*

Silk Ribbon Embroidered Fern

Use an 18" length of 4 mm wide silk ribbon embroidery ribbon in a #22 Chenille needle to do the "Pierced Leaf Stitch" (*Fancy Appliqué*, page 30). Take your first stitch at the top of the frond and work from side to side to the bottom of the frond.

PATTERN #5: "Cornucopia with Fruits and Acorns"

Type: Classic Baltimore

To make this block, refer to *Volume I*, Lesson 12.

Cornucopias, symbols of Abundance, were plentiful in the Baltimore Album Quilts. This one was made for Captain George W. Russell in 1852 and is from an Album Quilt in the Baltimore Museum of Art. My theory is that cornucopias in links of red, yellow, and blue as this one is, are Odd Fellow symbols of all the blessings bestowed upon us. In Odd Fellow iconography the "three links" represent Friendship, Love, and Truth. The symbolic colors for these are yellow, red, and blue. Captain Russell's blessings include the symbolic acorns for longevity.

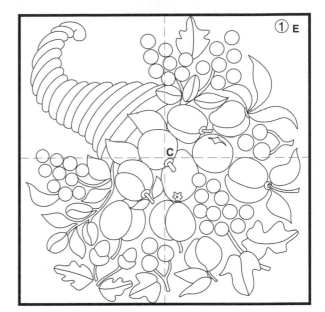

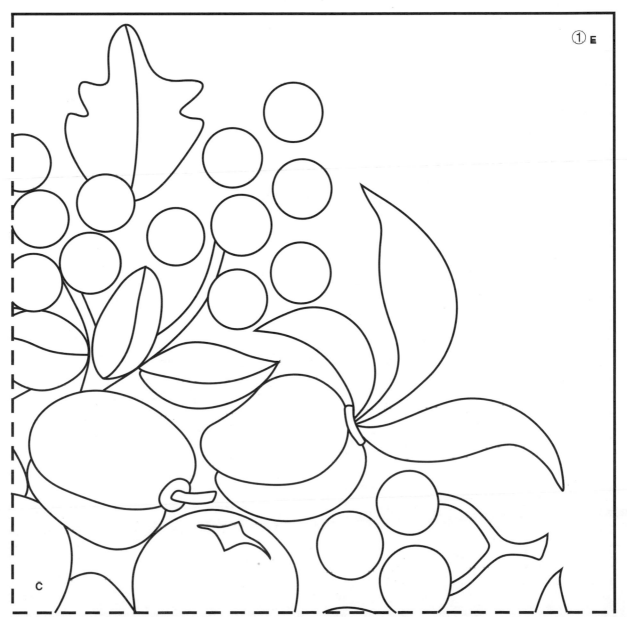

PATTERN #5: "Cornucopia with Fruits and Acorns"

Second Page

PATTERN #5: "Cornucopia with Fruits and Acorns"

Third Page

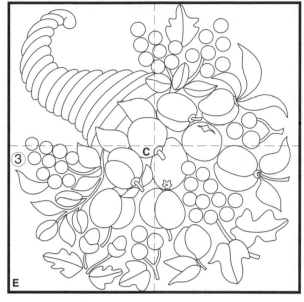

PATTERN #5: "Cornucopia with Fruits and Acorns"

Fourth Page

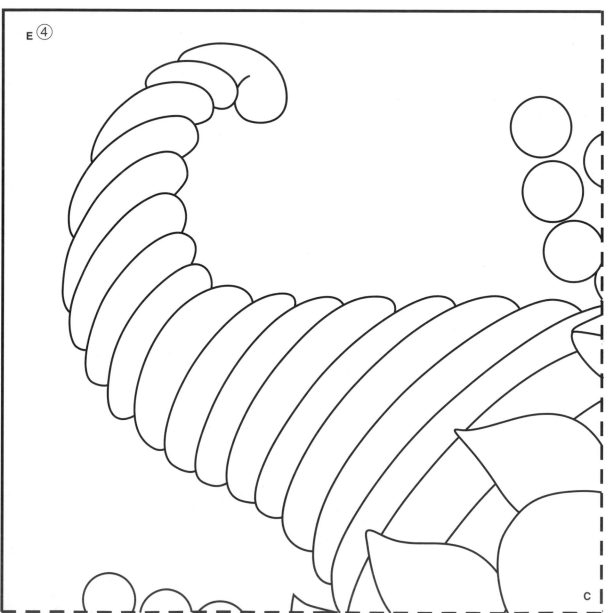

PATTERN #6: "The Rose of Sharon"

Type: Classic Baltimore

To make this block, refer to *Volume I*, Lessons 4, 5, 9.

This precise, symmetrical rose wreath may be among the earliest blocks in the Album Quilt collections and seems to predate the peak of the Baltimore Album Period. This version is from an 1843-45 Album. My Ribbon Appliqué version is pictured on the back cover and shows how a simple pattern suits turn-of-the-20th-21st century fancywork adaptation. The fancywork methods I used are outlined in *Romancing Ribbons into Flowers* and *Fancy Appliqué*.

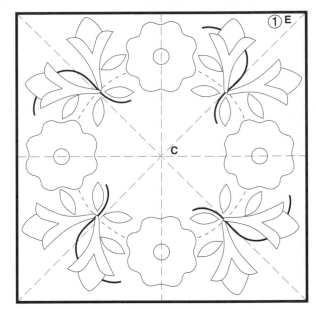

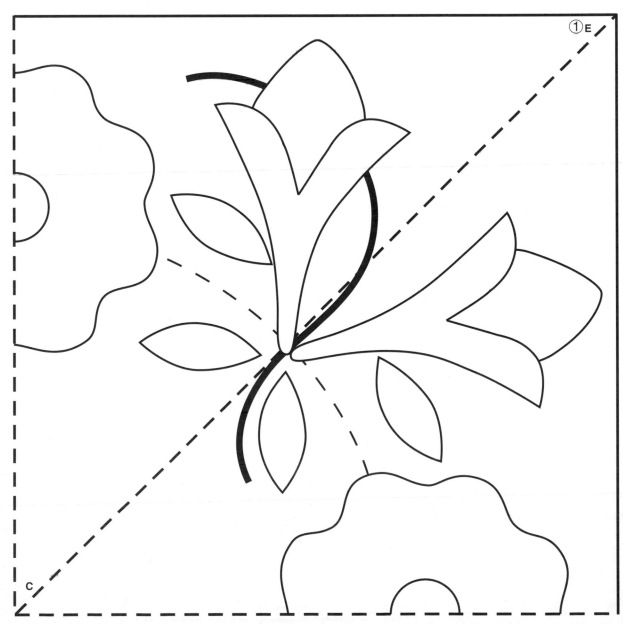

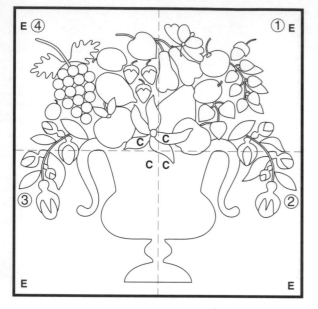

PATTERN #7: "Classic Urn for Fruit or Flowers"

Type: Classic Baltimore

To make this block, refer to *Volume I*, Lesson 12.

This urn is pictured in a block in the color section of *Papercuts and Plenty* (color plate 11, page 60) and is given here for the first time. The original is made in the shaded "rainbow" fabric of old Baltimore and filled with dimensionally shaded fruit. Why not take fruit shapes from other patterns in this compendium, then stencil-shade them with Craypas Specialist oil pastels to the kind of realism seen in the Bread and Wine block? The "Specialist" designation marks the highest oil content in Sakura's Craypas line. Heat-set, they work beautifully in this sort of art quilt.

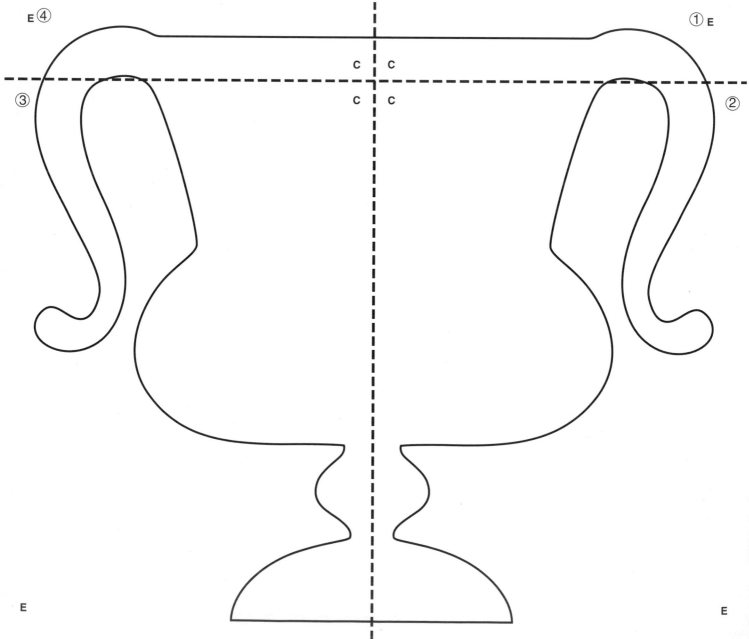

Index to the *Baltimore Beauties* Series Patterns and Techniques

Key to books listed in the Index. Book abbreviations are followed by the page number. Patterns included in this volume are preceded by a star (★).

AP12 =Appliqué 12 Easy Ways!

BorMed =Appliqué 12 Borders 7 Medallions

BAQ = Baltimore Album Quilts, the Pattern Companion to Baltimore Beauties and Beyond, Volume 1

BAR = Baltimore Album Revival!

DA = Dimensional Appliqué

DABAQ =Design a Baltimore Album Quilt!

SWAW = Spoken Without a Word

Vol. I =Baltimore Beauties and Beyond, Volume 1

Vol. II = Baltimore Beauties and Beyond, Volume 2

Vol. III = Papercuts and Plenty, Baltimore Beauties and Beyond, Volume 3

BOB = The Best of Baltimore Beauties

Key to type of pattern:

B = "Beyond" Baltimore, a quilt or block pattern beyond Baltimore in time or space

C = Classic Baltimore, a quilt or block pattern taken from a Baltimore Album quilt of the 19th century

P = Papercut or "Snowflake" pattern

S = Baltimore-style pattern, a quilt or block pattern that looks like a mid-19th century quilt but has uncertain provenance

T = Traditional Appliqué pattern (not Baltimore-Style), whether antique or contemporary

THE PATTERNS

THE TECHNIQUES

ABOUT THE AUTHOR

Elly Sienkiewicz has written fifteen important needlework books. Ten of these books comprise the Baltimore Beauties® series, begun in 1989. Elly places a complex historical style—the Baltimore-style Album Quilts—within the grasp of every late 20th century quiltmaker through her clear instruction and authentic patterns. Her leadership sustains this revival, now seventeen years strong. In a linked fellowship, those who love this style have taken it to something clearly "Beyond Baltimore."

Elly's path from career woman to stay-at-home mom of three, led her to become an early professional in the nascent quilt movement of the early 70s. Elly notes that her Wellesley College Class of 1964 is a "cusp generation"—women who as freshmen expected to live their mothers' 1950s societal ideal, but who were the object of radically different expectations by the time they graduated. Elly herself earned a Masters of Science degree and taught high school for seven years. A history major with a lifetime love of needleart, Elly's traditionalist desire to stay at home once her children arrived led to home-centered enterprises related to the burgeoning quilt world industry. Her experiences range from quilting teacher, to retail mail-order proprietess, to respected quiltmaker, to author, historian, and president of the Elly Sienkiewicz Appliqué Academy. Elly's devotion as a teacher, her concern for her students, and her love for quiltmaking have made her a cherished mentor. She lives in Washington, DC with her husband Stan, and, whenever they can be there too, their children Alex, Katya, and Donald and wife Katja and Elly's granddaughter, Little Ellie.

Fifteen books by Elly Sienkiewicz

Appliqué 12 Borders and Medallions
Appliqué 12 Easy Ways!
Appliqué Paper Greetings!
Baltimore Album Legacy
Baltimore Album Quilts
Baltimore Album Revival
Baltimore Beauties and Beyond, Vol. I
Baltimore Beauties and Beyond, Vol. II

Design a Baltimore Album Quilt
Dimensional Appliqué
Fancy Appliqué
Papercuts and Plenty, Baltimore Beauties and Beyond, Vol. III
Romancing Ribbons into Flowers
Spoken Without a Word
The Best of Baltimore Beauties

For a complete listing of C&T titles send for a free catalog from:

C&T Publishing, Inc.
P.O. Box 1456
Lafayette, CA 94549
800-284-1114
http://www.ctpub.com
email:ctinfo@ctpub.com

For Quilting Supplies contact:

Cotton Patch Mail Order
3405 Hall Lane, Dept. CTB
Lafayette, Ca 94549
email: quiltusa@yahoo.com
Web: www.quiltusa.com
800-835-4418
925-283-7883